"The Spirit of Cinco de Mayo"

✳

by Nathan Muncaster

Order this book online at www.trafford.com
or email orders@trafford.com

Most Trafford titles are also available at major online book retailers.

© Copyright 2009 Mark Muncaster.
All rights reserved. No part of this publication may be reproduced, stored in a retrieval system, or transmitted, in any form or by any means, electronic, mechanical, photocopying, recording, or otherwise, without the written prior permission of the author.

Note for Librarians: A cataloguing record for this book is available from Library and Archives Canada at www.collectionscanada.ca/amicus/index-e.html

Printed in Victoria, BC, Canada.

ISBN: 978-1-4269-1184-2 (sc)

Our mission is to efficiently provide the world's finest, most comprehensive book publishing service, enabling every author to experience success. To find out how to publish your book, your way, and have it available worldwide, visit us online at www.trafford.com

Trafford rev. 9/2/2009

 www.trafford.com

North America & international
toll-free: 1 888 232 4444 (USA & Canada)
phone: 250 383 6864 ♦ fax: 812 355 4082

Co-edited by Carol Buckley and Kathleen Pratt.
Special thanks to Michael Hogan, a mentor.
Dedicated to my parents – who believed in me.

Author's Note

This text is the culmination of my effort to portray a story that indirectly impacted American history greatly, yet the majority of Americans are unaware of it. Likewise, this subject is only superficially understood in Mexico and there is a dearth of materials on it in Mexico. It was written in an attempt to increase awareness of both American and Mexican readers alike and showed multiple perspectives. This is one of the reasons it was written in omniscient style. Lastly, it depicts a "snapshot" of the world as it was during and slightly after the US Civil War.

Research was conducted through primary sources such as Mexican historical archives, Mexican military records, site visits, as well as English language and other non-English language sources for the European events. However, in conducting this research I found that, at times, versions differed as to soldier quantities, last name spellings, event dates or even ranks. Certainly there were different perspectives on the various events. Known events were often elaborated with a writer's imagination and, in several cases, a few fictitious events were portrayed to liven the story. Nevertheless, this historical fiction story has been compiled with the best possible attention to detail in a manner that is enjoyable to the reader.

THE PROTAGONIST AND THE WORLD

April 20, 1861

Emperor Charles Louis-Napoléon Bonaparte III sat in his study in the château of Saint-Cloud. The room was truly opulent; the writing table at which he sat was topped with black marble fitted in gold brackets at the corners and supported on lavishly worked legs. The back frame around the cushion was inlaid with gilt and the legs were elegantly carved with precise groove work to accentuate their sheen.

On the table was a golden inkstand with a Baccarat crystal receptacle containing the finest writing ink. A gilded lid with an imperial eagle for a handle opened and closed the inkwell, a reminder of the glory days of his uncle's régime. A bejeweled snuffbox with a tiny silver spoon was adjacent to the inkwell as were multiple paperweights of quartz and semiprecious stones. There were no chairs in front of the writing table because no one could sit in his presence without an express invitation.

In front of the table, at a perpendicular angle, a plush red sofa with a gilded frame was arranged next to a coffee-table of oriental teakwood with Limoges porcelain coffee cups on top. This table was the only exception to the rule of décor in this room; the rest was true to the imperial style of the Second Empire. On the walls hung paintings depicting battle scenes of his uncle's Continental victories from the first decade of the century. He, Napoléon III, was almost on top of the world and where his uncle had fallen short on the Continent, he aspired to succeed in the entire world. He had reason to feel self-satisfied he told himself; today was his fifty-third birthday and much of the globe was at his beck and call.

He stood and stared outside the glass-paned doors to gaze at the expansive gardens. Countless servants moved through the trees and shrubs, meticulously clipping and trimming them into shapes and arches to be the stage of the world. And as well it should be!

In Asia the Tricolore had flown alongside the Union flag the prior year in the campaign to subjugate once again the Qing dynasty of Chine. After the burning of the Yuan Ming Yuan, the emperor Qianlong's summer palace, yet more trade concessions had been granted to the Europeans and les Anglais were at liberty to bleed the Chinese by selling them opium.

In Indo-Chine French encroachment on the old lands of Camboia, Cochinchine and Tonquin progressed slowly yet surely. Soon they would engulf Siam. In the South Pacific the protectorates of Polynesia were stable and the populating of Nouvelle Calédonie as a penal colony, based on the British model in Australia, was well under way.

In Africa, work on the Suez Canal, which had commenced two years ago, continued; a tribute to the supremacy of French engineering. When his program with the navy was complete, they would rival the British across the globe! The defeat of Trafalgar would be avenged. Algérie remained firmly in their grasp and they persisted in nibbling inwards from the West African coast at Libreville, flanked by other European powers.

On the Continent he held the Italians in check by force from their objective of absorbing the Patrimony of Saint Peter, home to

His Holiness Pope Pius IX and former seat of the Roman Empire. This was despite their recent unification under Vittorio Emmanuele owing to the military efforts of Garibaldi. The Austro-Hungarians, who had lost lands in the recent Italian revolution, seemed more focused on card games in the salons of Schönbrunn Palace with the traveling gamesters rather than on empire building and were still recovering from their expulsion by him from the Italian peninsula. In the east the Russians still licked their wounds from the Crimean War of five years' past and the Northern Countries and Iberia were tranquil. In the Levant the Druses in Syrie were passive.

But it was the Americas that captured the Emperor's imagination at this time. The Americans had, after years of squabbling and beating one another up in their congress, fragmented into civil war merely eight days ago. An American, a Monsieur Beauregard, presumably of French heritage by the name, had opened fire on a U.S. fort in the southern state of South Carolina. A tremendous opportunity of historical proportions now presented itself. Any imbecile could see that, if left unchecked, the Americans would one day rival France and England for hegemony. But divided… already envoys from both sides courted his diplomats. This must be exploited.

To their south was Mexico. Crippled from a recent civil war, the Mexican government could barely make interest payments on what it owed foreign bankers. An invasion of Mexico under the screen of an American civil war in direct violation of that policy the American government had proclaimed, the Monroe Doctrine, would give France a foothold in the Americas to check further American expansion and reestablish colonies. Although Louisiane, sold by his uncle fifty-five years ago for war funds, was irretrievable, they could still march south, linking to their penal colony in Guyane. The former Spanish colonies were in such a shambles anyway they would never be able to resist his version of the First Empire's La Grande Armée.

The Emperor clenched his fist in front him.

This would have to be done in a manner that did not antagonize or menace the British or other European powers as a whole. An overt invasion would never do. His previous effort, a filibustering expedition of 260 Frenchmen in the state of Sonora in 1852 had been a complete failure. Although the landing in Guaymas had been undertaken with the backing of the Mexican president, ostensibly to protect the Mexican miners from Apache Indian attacks, it had concluded several years later with the execution of its leader, the late Compte de Raousset-Boulbon.

He needed a pretense, something the other Europeans would agree to.

The Emperor's mind searched.

THE BIG DREAMER

June 4, 1861

As Juan Antonio looked around at his surroundings, the hated army of the Conservatives was in flight, routed by the Constitutionalist army led by Generals Ignacio Zaragoza and Jesús González Ortega. Hundreds of yards away, enemy soldiers dropped their rifles and abandoned their cannons without spiking them before the intrepid Constitutionalist advance. The field at Silao had been won, the Constitutionalists were victorious and González Ortega, hero of the state of Zacatecas, had shone with valor and was forever indebted to him, Juan Antonio, his most loyal soldier for saving his life during the battle...

It had been so sudden – the coundercharge against the Conservative attack that Ortega's vanguard had been caught out ahead of the lines. Driven by a desperate courage, Juan Antonio fired one rifle then a second and, reaching for a third he saw General Ortega beset by two opponents. He was valiantly parrying their rifle thrusts with his saber but in time he would be overcome.

Yelling madly, Juan Antonio pulled his knife from his belt and grappled with one soldier, stabbing him in the ribs on the way to the ground. The man gasped and clutched Juan Antonio's arm and chin, trying to stop the inevitable deathblow that the young Juan Antonio would deliver.

Knocking his opponent's arm out of the way, Juan Antonio drove the blade into the soldier's chest. Not wasting time on the man's fading expression of horror Juan Antonio spun around to see the second enemy leveling his rifle at General Ortega who had stumbled over a corpse and was rising from the ground.

In a fluid motion Juan Antonio threw the knife into the side of the enemy's belly. The man let his rifle fall to the earth and grasped his wound, dropping to his knees. Fully recovered, General Ortega slashed the soldier across the chest with his saber then back again on his neck. The man fell, lifeless.

General Ortega's eyes showed recognition that Juan Antonio had courageously saved his life. Around them, rallying Constitutionalists were running headfirst into the enemy ranks and driving them back. The rest of the battle passed like a dream as Juan Antonio, emboldened by the admiration of his adored General Ortega, fought valiantly and unhesitatingly…

Now the Conservatives were routed and he, Juan Antonio, hero of Silao, savior of General Ortega, steadfast Juarista in the Guerra de la Reforma – the Reform War – would take his place among the elite of Presidente Juárez's men. He and González Ortega: Constitutionalists, patriots, Mexicans…

The tolling of the church bell aroused Juan Antonio from his reverie. Around him the summer heat baked the outlying hills and, in the distant sunny flatlands below lay his hometown of San Luis Potosí. Three birds flew above him; he wondered if they'd believed him to be dead and had hoped to feed on him. "No," he said to them internally, "not dead, just daydreaming."

He disliked it when something disturbed his midmorning siesta on his day off, especially when he was interrupted on the verge of doing something truly glorious like defending México from a fictitious return of General Santa Anna or leading a campaign to take back the ceded northern provinces from the norteamericanos.

A second bell began tolling in discord with the first. Now a third started, that must be all the iglesias, the Cathedral, San Francisco and Carmen combined! The sound seemed like a loud clanging that carried into the hills where he had been dozing. With all the bells ringing there was certain to be important news. And when there was important news people always gathered to discuss the implications afterward in the Hotel America where Juan Antonio worked as a table boy. If he were late for the crowd he would certainly be punished, even though this was his day off. Shaking the drowsiness from his limbs, Juan Antonio began to run toward the town of San Luis Potosí as fast as he could, which, as an athletic youth of eighteen, was pretty swiftly.

TRAUMATIC NEWS

June 4, 1861

The run back to the town took some time, but the arid heat of high summer had not started yet and Juan Antonio enjoyed the exercise. Once he had left the foothills it was a flat run all the way to the outskirts of town.

San Luis Potosí, with its narrow streets and Spanish-style iglesias, always seemed to be at the center of critical events. México was undergoing turbulent times and Juan Antonio had never known anything but unrest in his country. It was here that Juan Antonio had peered out past the barred windows of their red painted house near the Plaza de San Francisco to watch General Santa Anna parade in the city at the head of twenty thousand soldiers with General Ampudia in the cold winter of 1846.

As a young boy in the times immediately after the expulsion of Santa Anna he would listen to his father talk with Ponciano Arriaga about the new era of hope for the Estados Unidos Mexicanos.

Mr. Arriaga and his father were childhood friends and Juan Antonio never grew tired of his stories about the tobacco factory in New Orleans where he had worked in exile with two other Constitutionalists, Benito Juárez and Melchor Ocampo. Ponciano Arriaga was a close of friend of the current presidente, Benito Juárez and the former minister of government, Melchor Ocampo. Ponciano Arriaga had been the first signer of the Carta Fundamental of 1857, drafted in the Palacio del Gobierno in San Luis Potosí.

It was through Juan Antonio's family's friendship with Señor Ortega that he had been fortunate enough to be allowed to serve as a page to the hero of Zacatecas, General Ortega, in the Guerra de la Reforma in the winter of 1858-1859 and later.

During this time, when San Luis Potosí had been occupied by the Conservatives and the previous governor of Zacatecas had fled, his family had relocated to stay with an aunt of Señor Arriaga who in turn introduced them to the then new governor of Zacatecas, General Jesús González Ortega.

Juan Antonio had seen the Juaristan army defeat the forces of the hated General Joaquin Miramón and followed the men as they retook San Luis Potosí on March 23rd, 1859. Juan Antonio knew that he was fortunate just to have been taken along on these missions, because even the pages and gun-cleaning boys endured hardships and danger. Only after exposure and demonstrated courage could he feel as if he had done his duty and matured to manhood.

While his family had stayed in San Luis Potosí after its recapture to repair the damage done to their home during the Conservative occupation Juan Antonio had continued on as a volunteer page and was able to see the tremendous victory of Generals Ortega and Zaragoza at Silao on August 10th, 1860. Juan Antonio was present when Ortega declined both his first and second commission as brigadier general – he, a man with no formal military training who had become a respected military leader by virtue of his courage and determination.

Juan Antonio was winded by the time he reached the town proper. As the narrow cobbled streets, framed by the square houses with wrought-iron balconies and identical facades, led him to the garden of the Iglesia de San Carmen the bells stopped. Juan Antonio was sure to miss the announcement and would have to rely on what his friends would tell him. It would be awful to appear uninformed when his friends gathered at their houses to discuss politics or when they came to the Hotel America to talk with him.

"Juan Antonio, don't kill yourself! It's a telegram, they'll post it later."

It was Graciana, their neighbor from the Plaza de San Francisco who helped the priests in Templo de San Francisco.

The priests of San Luis were good men, according to his father, more concerned with the fate of their congregations and the future of the country then with the amassing of property for the Catholic Church and resistance to the Ley Lerdo, the Lerdo Law, meant to redistribute the more than one third of land owned by the Catholic Church to the Mexican people.

"Do you know what it is?" Juan Antonio asked.

"No, but you come and tell me later! I'll be waiting!"

Smiling and waving goodbye, Juan Antonio continued on his way.

The streets, normally occupied by citizens conducting their daily chores, were empty as the townspeople were all in the Plaza de Armas. As he drew closer to the plaza he could hear cries of shock and dismay at what was certain to be bad tidings announced by the crier. Certainly it would be something to do with the norteamericanos, their Civil War had started two months ago and everyone expected the slave states to use the war as a pretext to take more land from México.

Or maybe the news would be about the banditos in the south?

From the Cathedral the crowd of people extended out of the Plaza de Armas and back along its south wall. Juan Antonio didn't recognize anyone nearby and would have to locate his friends later. Coming to a halt behind the mass of townsfolk he could just barely see the crier in the stand and make out what he was announcing.

"Faithful Constitutionalist, former minister of government, devoted literary supporter and beloved Mexican patriot we pray that your soul is at peace and thank you for your selfless contributions to our beloved homeland. I ask that we all, in these turbulent times, pray for our respected Melchor Ocampo, who loved so much to see his people happy."

The crowd was silent but Juan Antonio could sense their acute anguish. Melchor Ocampo! How could Melchor Ocampo be dead? The Guerra de la Reforma was finished and Melchor Ocampo was a Juárez supporter of unquestioned merit. Could his death be of natural causes? Nobody important in México died of natural causes in these times. And there had been cries of shock earlier. What had happened?

"Go in peace and pray for our souls and our homeland." concluded the crier, after which he stepped down from the platform, folding the telegram as he descended. He appeared to be planning to keep it and wasn't going to post it in the square as was customarily done.

Well, Juan Antonio would find out what it contained soon enough in the Hotel America. There were bound to be thirsty people filling the tables, discussing current events. Knowing he would be needed at work Juan Antonio started to make his way through the stunned crowd that was milling about and coalescing into smaller groups. On his way through, Juan Antonio overheard enough conversation to understand that Melchor Ocampo had been tried and summarily executed in the same day. It could not possibly be Presidente Juárez who had done this! That was impossible; such a heinous betrayal could never originate from the mind of that man. But then who?

He spotted his friend Garcia with two of his other friends. They looked upset and were conversing animatedly. Juan Antonio made his way over to them.

"Is it true? Ocampo is dead?" Juan Antonio asked.

"They killed him." Juan replied. He was a tall boy with darker skin than most Mexicans due to the absence of any criollo blood in his ancestry.

"Just murdered him," Garcia added, "Shot him then hung him from a tree. It was Leonardo Márquez, the Conservative general. They sent a Spaniard in with a posse and they kidnapped him and killed him. Shot him dead."

"Juárez won't stand for this; he'll send General Ortega." Juan Antonio stared excitedly.

"No," Garcia replied "not Ortega. He is no longer war minister. They said that Juárez sent Santos Degollado and Leonardo Valle."

"Well that makes sense." Juan Antonio said. "General Ortega is fighting together with Juárez and Degollado has always been a key military chief under Juárez.

Where did they do this?" he asked.

Diego, the most timid of the boys with pale criollo skin and a big nose from his Basque ancestors piped in, "At his hacienda. They just rode in, took him hostage, had a same-day trial and shot him, all yesterday. They took him from Michoacán to Hidalgo to execute him."

"The worst part is no one stopped them." Juan said. "They must have ridden for hours on the roads."

The weight of the news was starting to sink in for Juan Antonio. "There is no justice, there must be justice!" he said. "How can this happen to so close an ally of the Presidente, by the same people who lost the Guerra de los Tres Años – the Three Years' War – so brazenly?"

After a brief awkward pause Garcia said flatly "The government has no money, it is too weak. The banditos are stronger and they pay off the army."

"It has to stop." The other boys were surprised to hear Diego speak so passionately.

Juan Antonio, not wanting to be overcome by pessimism, said "I think it will now, finally. We won the Guerra de la Reforma, even with all the European governments supporting the Conservatives and the church paying money to their army, we won. I think Juárez can focus on wiping out the last of Santa Anna's loyalists, the banditos, all of them. It will get better."

"Hey. What were you doing to miss the telegram anyway?" Garcia asked Juan Antonio.

"I was relaxing in the hills."

"Planning being a general?"

"No, not I. That would take too long. Besides, I would have to defeat big armies over years and years to be a general. Take General Ortega, he just kept winning and winning even though he was outnumbered and underequipped. But he did it by inspiring his troops to keep fighting. I saw the way he spoke with them, organizing them. The Conservative soldiers never seemed to care much; they just got paid to fight."

"How do you know how they fought? You were never in the fighting!" interjected Diego.

"That was because they didn't let me. I wanted to fight, I didn't care if I got wounded or even killed because in me, in my heart I wanted to fight and I was prepared to die!"

"Well the war's over so unless we take back Alta California you won't have to." As he spoke Garcia patted Juan Antonio on the shoulder. "Are you going to serve drinks at the hotel now?"

"Yes. Do you muchachos want to come?"

"No, but tell me tonight what they say. You can knock on my shutter, it doesn't matter how late."

"Sure, I'll tell you tonight then. See you!" Juan Antonio said, waving and turning away.

The square had not emptied much, but it was now possible to walk uninhibited from one point to another. The townspeople had split off into smaller groups of acquaintances and were talking among themselves the same way that Juan Antonio and his friends had just spoken. Looking over at the Hotel America he saw it had mostly filled up and he was certain his father would be there, talking with his associates and the owner of the hotel, Señor Santiago.

He walked over to the saloon because this was the best place to hear the real news. His father's friends always seemed to know more than the people in the plaza, and they would let him ask questions and were friendly to him.

Pushing open the swinging wooden half-doors Juan Antonio could see the saloon was full and everyone was talking animatedly either at the tables or standing between them. But nobody took notice of his entry, not even Señor Santiago who was so busy he could not even glance up.

Grabbing some of the dirty shot glasses on the tables Juan Antonio worked his way to the back room to grab a rag and a tray. The empty back room meant Santiago and Benito Juárez would be upstairs or tending to the customers.

Peering over the swinging doors from the back Juan Antonio spotted his father at one of the tables, seated with his usual colleagues – Ponciano Arriaga, Jesús Garza, a dry goods merchant and Victor Ramirez, a former soldier in the Juaristan army who now farmed on the outskirts of town. With any luck, they would talk longer than the rest of the customers as usual and eventually Juan Antonio would be allowed to sit with them. But for now, the customers would want their tequila.

TALKING TO THE RIGHT PEOPLE

June 4, 1861

After most of the customers had left and the lamps had been lit, Señor Santiago signaled that Juan Antonio could sit with his father and friends. He picked up a chair from an adjacent table and raised his eyebrows at his father, who moved over to make a place for him at the table beside him.

"Come, come my son." Francisco Ayala, his father, said. "We were waiting for your opinion on what has happened."

"I heard that Leonardo Márquez sent a Spanish mercenary to Ocampo's hacienda and that they kidnapped him and shot him." Juan Antonio said. "Is this correct?"

"Yes, and they left him dangling from a tree."

"I think it's horrible and that they should hang Márquez."

"Good opinion, boy." Jesús Garza said. "They already sent two of Melchor Ocampo's closest friends, Generals Leonardo Valle and Santos Degollado to prosecute him. Juárez grants amnesty to this man – this half man – and he repays that leniency by murdering one of Juárez's closest associates? He will hang in México and burn in hell!"

Ponciano Arriaga cleared his throat and spoke calmly. "Yes, God willing. But it is not so easy for the Juaristas to bring men like Márquez to justice. The government is so indebted, so poor; we can barely pay meager salaries to a skeleton bureaucracy, much less pay and equip an army to clear the countryside of the remnants of Santa Anna loyalists, banditos and strongmen. Presidente Juárez has already declared our foreign debt to be unpayable, a sum equivalent to decades of our annual receipts.

"The majority we owe to the British but we also owe to the Spanish as well as some money to the French and norteamericanos."

"You would think that the norteamericanos would relate more to us, coming from similar origins and having fought the same struggle for independence from Europe as we did. In the beginning they were vulnerable also, invaded by the British while we fought for our independence from Spain. They are a proud people, you must say, and I always wonder if ever our nations can work together for a common American destiny. But, for that, they would need to forget their notion of Manifest Destiny."

"But, won't the norteamericanos loan us money?" Juan Antonio asked. "The war between us is over and they got to the Pacific. We buy many of their printing presses and lamps – and they have their Monroe Doctrine to protect the Western Hemisphere from European interference, right?"

His father shook his head. "A sword has two edges, my son. At one time the norteamericanos intervened in Veracruz to attack the Conservative navy and save Presidente Juárez. But that was then, this is now."

Ramirez, who had listened with the attentiveness of a soldier who has seen much and learned not to make bold statements until he was sure of his thoughts, finally spoke. "Nothing is free, Juan Antonio, and the noretamericanos will want something from us. I want to be their friend, but in troubled times friends are few and far between."

This brought a moment of silence to the table, and Juan Antonio paused to consider his surroundings. There were only a few more tables with guests, and one of them was in the process of paying Señor Santiago.

When he turned his attention back to his table, he noticed Señor Ramirez was looking at him in a manner that was both affectionate and knowing. His dark bushy eyebrows framed his eyes and his big black mustache contrasted dramatically against his olive skin.

As Juan Antonio peered into Ramirez's eyes, he searched for the answers to the questions all idealistic young men have; what is manhood? What is truth? What is friendship? For now Juan Antonio didn't have the answers but he hoped that this recent tragedy could lead to another military campaign against General Márquez. Then Juan Antonio, older than he was at the battle of Silao last summer, would get a chance to find the answers to the questions on the battlefield; at the point where right meets wrong and truth is unclouded.

As the conversation resumed, Ramirez broke his gaze, leaving Juan Antonio free to daydream…

Were these four men not friends? Arriaga had sent him to Ortega and arranged for him to work directly for the general. Wasn't that friendship?

The men were talking now about México's financial difficulties; how the redistribution and sale of church land under the Ley Lerdo should have resolved this; how the embezzlement of the treasury by Santa Anna had bankrupted México; how the sale of land to the norteamericanos was for too little; an act of pure treason and avarice by Santa Anna; how banditos inhibited commerce; how the French provoked the "Guerra de los Pasteles" – the Bakery War – of 1838 so they could steal from México.

His mind drifted off again…

How could a soldier question comradeship? Was not the bond formed under fire the strongest bond of all? Was he not a friend of General Ortega, for whom he had served and for whom he would lay down his life? How could a veteran question friendship?

Now Juan Antonio's thoughts wandered to his friends Juan, Garcia and Diego, as well as Graciana. He might still be able to tell them all that he heard tonight, if it were not too late.

Excusing himself he got up from the table, and taking as many empty glasses and mugs as he could carry, he went to the bar where Señor Santiago was leaning against the back of the bar with both forearms, listening to them.

Juan Antonio asked if he could leave if all his chores were done and Señor Santiago consented. He was a nice boss, especially since his father and his friends gathered here several times a week. Juan Antonio set to pushing in all the chairs and resetting tables and was able to finish organizing the bar in twenty minutes. With that he said "Buenas noches" to his father and his friends and stepped out of the Hotel America into the warm, moonlit night of San Luis Potosí.

July 1861

The next few weeks passed somewhat slowly for Juan Antonio. It was summer and consequently he was busy in the evenings working in the Hotel America. His friends, as always, had been very curious to hear what the adults were saying, especially since Señor Arriaga always seemed to know what Presidente Juárez's intentions were. Listening to the older men on their evenings drinking tequila together was an excellent way for Juan Antonio to anticipate future events.

As it turned out, fate was not kind to the Juarista generals who had set out to settle the matter of Melchor Ocampo's murder. Both of them were ambushed and killed by Leonardo Márquez. Retribution would have to wait as the Juárez government, fresh from the end of a grueling civil war, could not afford to pursue its enemies at this time.

This deeply upset the townspeople, because San Luis Potosí was cradle to the Constitutional cause and the Carta Fundamental, which guaranteed freedom of expression, and its citizens sympathized with Presidente Juárez. But in a time when the federal government could not even make interest payments to its European creditors such concerns had to be made secondary.

Juan Antonio and his friends, especially Garcia, talked of enlisting in the army and fighting for the security and glory of México. This would be difficult because the government could not pay for the soldiers' equipment and wages, but somehow their parents would afford a rifle for them and they would be able to get by.

One late morning, while Juan Antonio was helping his father to clean his rifle, an old revolver rifle from 1852, Juan Antonio, as young men aspiring to manhood will often do, asked his father if he could enlist and help the government to eradicate the banditos plaguing the southern hill country. His father's reply was subdued.

"Well, I imagine one day you will do so of your own accord but for now you should wait until the government conscripts the men of this town."

"But father, if I could just volunteer for General Ortega in Zacatecas he would put me in a good position and treat me well."

'Yes, I'm sure he would." his father replied. "However, for now the government isn't going to pay for a general conscription like that. I wish they would, because what México needs right now is a strong, stable government and an end to internal strife. The diablos who steal on the highways and in the hills should be hunted down and hung with no clemency. Some townspeople can't even work their fields for fear of being slain, and they spend all day scanning the horizon for bandits and all night praying to make it through until morning. The worst part is; I'm sure many of these banditos could live decently as honest citizens. And if the government doesn't stop them, they will form countries and we'll end up worse then we were under Santa Anna!"

Thoughts of the disintegration of the United Provinces of South America came to Juan Antonio's mind when his father said this. He hesitated, as he was nervous about making his next request.

"Father, I would like your permission to enlist with General Ortega. I know he'll treat me well and see to it that I can serve my country with honor. And, with this rifle nobody would have to pay for my weapon."

His father had predicted this request as early as the previous year. He was both proud and protective of his son. Ever since their dislocation from San Luis Potosí and their subsequent time spent in Zacatecas he had witnessed his son's increasing idolization of the soldiers. The Zacatecan soldiers under General Ortega's command were good men, and he was extremely fortunate that his son had survived and matured greatly under Jesús González Ortega's shadow. Yet, he wished his son could realize that, in this day and age, his trials of manhood would be forced upon him anyway and there was no need to seek danger prematurely.

"Juan Antonio, your mother and I have already discussed that you cannot enlist unless there is another national crisis, like the Guerra de la Reforma. We were blessed to have survived that unscathed and you are our only son. You have already given much to your country and you will soon be called to contribute more. You are respected by your friends and fellow citizens."

"But the war criminals go unpunished."

"Yes, indeed. But their time will come. Ponciano Arriaga was saying that Presidente Juárez is going to negotiate a suspension of our foreign debt payments with the European bankers. With the money we save, Juárez will be able to pay for troops to move into the countryside to eliminate the banditos and we can have peace. And maybe you can enlist then, properly. If you enlist without a war, you will just end up starving, with or without Jesús González Ortega."

"I wouldn't starve."

"You'd probably come close to it. Regardless, no good could come of it. I am sure that one day you will have to fight for what is yours. Why rush that day when it is probably inevitable? I know you're a man." He patted Juan Antonio on the shoulder. "Here, give me the rifle and I'll finish cleaning it. It just makes you think of war. Why don't you go walking with Garcia?'

"All right then. I'll be back in time to help with dinner."

With that Juan Antonio put down the rifle he had been cleaning, handed the oily rags back to his father and walked out into the summer air.

It was almost midday and there was hardly any shade from the walls of the Templo de San Francisco close by. He did not recognize anybody in the Plaza de San Francisco which was at the end of his street so he just passed through without stopping to talk and continued toward the Plaza de Armas.

The heat reflecting from the cobblestones in the street felt good to Juan Antonio. It was still not high summer and the heat was invigorating to him. The colors of the houses were highlighted by the piercing mountain sunlight; first yellow, then reddish brown and burnt orange and then white. The Potosinos were a people who took pride in the upkeep of their homes and gardens.

Most of the window shutters were closed so Juan Antonio couldn't see inside the homes. But occasionally one of the houses' shutters was open and he could see the residents inside, brewing coffee, cooking, or talking among themselves. In this part of México, the Potosinos preferred to place plants on the window ledges, since in the mountains they were not exposed to the desert heat and they helped to beautify the streets.

Entering the Plaza de Armas, Juan Antonio did not see Garcia there so instead he purchased a newspaper. Entering a store, he bought a copy of *El Siglo XIX*, then strolled toward the house where Garcia lived on the north side of town near the Mercado de Hidalgo.

The headlines spoke of the crushing debt the country owed to European creditors. There was a statement by Presidente Juárez on the matter that he would read with Garcia.

After greeting Garcia at his home, Juan Antonio and his friend decided to head back to the Plaza de Armas to read the newspaper together. Walking to the plaza Juan Antonio perceived again how tall Garcia was and how he always seemed to catch the eyes of the señoritas.

When they reached the plaza they sat down on a bench and began to read an article that described the massive amounts of money the government owed to, above all England, but also Spain, the United States of America, and France.

Because of the risk of insolvency, and because a large portion of the debt had been incurred by the Conservatives in power in México City during the Guerra de la Reforma, while Presidente Juárez had been trapped in Veracruz, Juárez had declared a two-year moratorium on debt payments and was in the process of negotiating for reduced interest rates. The rates that the Conservative had consented to in their final desperate months were absurd, and the Estados Unidos Mexicanos could barely make the interest payments. This had been ratified by Congreso. Evidently this had caused a huge uproar in Europe. In contrast, their northern neighbor was more concerned about its civil war and was disposed to negotiate.

Juan Antonio and Garcia sat talking about the events for a while. Both desired to become soldiers to leave their hometown, to see the rest of the country and chase banditos in ravines. With young boys their optimism overpowers their reason and little did they suspect they would soon have more than ample opportunity to prove themselves before Dios and country.

TROMPE D'OEUIL

October 15, 1861

Across the Atlantic, close to Paris a magnificent carriage carried the British ambassador to France to the palace of Versailles. Gilded ornamentation covered the front edges of the carriage and lanterns mounted on the corners reflected the clear sunlight. A red and gold emblem was emblazoned on the side doors of the shiny black carriage whose wheels rattled as it sped along the trails of rural France. The coachmen were seated on a fine red cushion, as was Lord Cowley, who peered out behind the felt curtains at the green grass and changing colors of the northern French autumn.

Already a chill was in the air and Lord Cowley rubbed his hands together as his mind raced over the events of the preceding months. The Mexican cessation of payments on July 17th had finally provided the pretext that England had been waiting for. Since the Mexicans' three year war, the British press, at the request of Her Majesty's Government, had publicly lauded a joint Anglo-French intervention to mediate the dispute between the Constitutionalists and Conservatives.

A Mexico dependent upon British capital, and subservient to its needs, would serve as an independent check to expanding American power. A Mexico ruled by a European installed puppet monarch could one day be used as an ally in any conflict against the United States and could serve as a port for the Royal Navy.

With the outbreak of the American civil war, the Yankees were powerless to enforce the Monroe Doctrine. France had secured the support of the expatriated Mexican Conservatives and Santa Anna loyalists and had successfully negotiated an excellent candidate to be emperor of Mexico.

Pulling his fob watch from his waistcoat, Lord Cowley realized he was running late. The negotiations were almost finished by now, and to arrive late risked a loss of prestige before the French, or worse, French secretary of foreign relations Thouvenel could take umbrage at his tardiness. Lord Cowley's demeanor must be perfect, his French flawless, his posture assertive and unyielding without overstepping his limitations.

He called to the coachman to make haste, and the coach began to jostle uncomfortably racing over the stony road.

French and Spanish military support was necessary in this undertaking but England must be certain that they did not exceed their usefulness. All of them entertained the reconquest of their colonies in the Americas but England required the legitimacy of multiple parties as well as the weight of the French military. One never knew if the United States would commit the resources to deflect this movement, even weakened by the recent Union defeat at Bull Run in Virginia.

Should France exceed the limits of the joint agreement, England could do little to stop them. Mexico owed France a paltry 3 million pounds to England's 70 million but Napoléon III dreamed of returning to the days of his uncle's expansionism. To this France had added a grossly overstated debt owed on the bonds pawned to the French investors by that Swiss scoundrel Jecker. He had loaned 3 million pounds sterling to Miguel Miramón toward the end of 1859 and then resold the note with interest for himself. Now the French clamored for 12 million pounds for a two year investment that was sealed with criminals and devils. These French just didn't understand risk and proper return... An Englishman would have never made the same investment!

The French ambitions seemed boundless. Their agents were conspiring to annex the territory south of Hong Kong and east of Siam in Cochinchina and to attach it to Saigon under the umbrella of their joint venture against the Annamese empire. France was even more brazen in its commerce with the secessionist southern states of America. And they challenged British interests around the globe. Yet the French controlled the relationships that were central in putting this deal together. Be it in China, Mexico, America or Greater India, Britain and France were bound together as distrustful allies in their quest for world dominion.

The present Mexican ambassador to France and ardent monarchist, José Hidalgo y Esnaurizar and the former Mexican ambassador to France General Almonte both assured Louis-Napoléon that the Mexican population would rise up in support of European assistance. Dubious – yet possible. At Compiègne the French had secured the Mexican monarchists' vows of support and were trying to organize a return of former president Santa Anna to Mexico as a figurehead. All of this served British interests as a guarantee of continued financial protection and the expansion of their interests in the Western Hemisphere.

Cowley heard the coachmen announce his arrival to the guards at the gates of Versailles and snapped out of his reverie, and he peered out his window at the baroque style palace beyond the black iron fence with gold seals cast in the center of the bars.

The palace was massive; hundreds of glass-paned windows faced out onto the large paved courtyard through which he would soon pass to the visitors' coach house to the left. Three stories high, the middle story façade was embellished with dozens of white columns and niches with classical statues. The roof had a parapet punctuated by literally hundreds of sculpted stone urns and coats of arms.

The carriage pulled forward again and the wheels clattered over the paving stones. He made himself ready, then grasped the small shiny leather case which contained the latest draft of the London Convention.

The coach stopped in front of the entry door and a French liveryman unfolded the coach's steps and opened the carriage door for him. Secrecy was important and it was the reason that the meeting was taking place in Versailles as opposed to Paris or Compiègne. The three countries' collusion, while public on paper, must have the luxury of confidentiality to negotiate the finer details of the arrangement.

"Merci." Cowley said as he descended to enter the foyer and awaited his reception.

His arrival was announced with the pomp and circumstance befitting a diplomat of his station. After approximately ten minutes' waiting time in the ornate foyer he was led through a hallway to the office where his counterpart, French Secretary of Foreign Relations Thouvenel, awaited him.

Every time Cowley visited Versailles he was struck by the ostentation of the French style; wallpaper with pastel backgrounds, flared chair arms with reflective silver plating, gilt clocks and gold filigree on everything, as well as countless statues and paintings whose sole purpose served exclusively to overwhelm the visitor. Reaching for his snuffbox, he delicately inhaled a tiny spoonful of snuff then entered the Appollon Salon as beckoned by the liveryman, who wore a pastel blue flowing coat with gold embroidery and a powdered wig.

"Bonjour, Lord Cowley." Thouvenel stood as Cowley entered the sunlit room.

"Good morning, Secretary Thouvenel." Cowley replied in French. "A pleasure to see you as always." Glancing at his surroundings Cowley was struck by the quantity of mirrors in the chamber. Mirrors, many mirrors embellished with golden ornamentation on the sides. He pondered whether or not this was an ironic parallel to diplomacy with the French; in dealing with the French, one never knew if you were dealing with the true image or just a reflection.

"Your journey was not too tiring, non?"

"Au contraire, I enjoyed the ride. Your country is most scenic this time of year, Secretary Thouvenel."

"You have brought the final draft from your parliament?"

"Indeed." With that, Cowley ceremoniously presented the case to Thouvenel, drawing back his arm with a flourish.

Thouvenel walked back to the writing table, opened the case and spread out the document. He spent several moments perusing it, and then turned back to Cowley and said, "Très bien – naturally, there will be minor modifications but I can imagine the Emperor will approve the project and pass it along to London and Madrid. England will be ready?"

"England will most certainly be ready. The *Times* and the *Morning Post* have been most judicious in their reporting of the chaos in Mexico, as well as the attempted forfeiture of their enormous debts to our countries and their persecutions of Englishmen on their soil."

"Bon – good – we count on the same support from the *Journal de Debates*." Thouvenel drew a deep breath and looked hard at Cowley. "And of England's intentions with Mexico?"

"Why the same as the Empire of France, Secretary Thouvenel – the guarantee of repayment of its loans and the arresting of American expansion in the Western Hemisphere."

"And England has no ulterior motives? No intent to keep its soldiers cantoned in Mexico for a future invasion of the United States? I must emphasize this is the Emperor's gravest worry, Lord Cowley."

"I can assure you, England seeks only to protect what is owed it and check the United States."

"Well, Lord Cowley, we need not worry too much as the Americans seem to be doing a good job of self destroying, non?"

"Yes, yes it would seem so."

"Then, Lord Cowley, if there is nothing else I must bid you adieu and discuss this immediately with the Emperor. I am instructed to advise you that, should there be no modifications of substance to this version we will forward it to Lord Russell in London directly as well as Señor Izturiz y Montero in Spain. You do understand, this is merely to expedite the matter."

"I wouldn't have it otherwise."

"Bon. I'm sure we will be seeing more of one another in the future. A good day to you."

Clicking his heels together and bowing curtly, Cowley bid Thouvenel farewell and departed Versailles.

After Cowley's departure Thouvenel studied the British counterproposal. There were no fundamental changes, just the routine final jostling for position. The English did not suspect anything!

Knowing that the Emperor would be strolling the palace gardens with his entourage, Thouvenel gathered the papers together and hurried to discuss them with him. Walking along the Grand Canal, he saw the group stopped next to some chairs among the sculptured shrubbery. Making his way to the Emperor along the geometric paths of the garden, he felt a rush of relief. Everything was moving in their favor; the dictator would be pleased.

As Thouvenel approached, the individuals surrounding the Emperor lowered their parasols and let him pass. The Emperor turned to face him, the collection of medals on his chest catching the sun for an instant.

Thouvenel bowed. "Your Highness, I have met with Lord Cowley and analyzed their most recent draft."

"What is your determination?" inquired Louis-Napoléon, twirling his handlebar mustache in a posture of aloof interest.

"No substantial modifications, just lesser requests for Your Highness's perusal."

"And do you think they know about our discussions with Maximilian?"

"I don't believe so, Your Highness. Our spies in their parliament tell me they are unaware."

"Excellent. Leave me the document. I'll study it and let you know."

Bowing grandly and flourishing his right arm beneath his chest while raising his left arm above his back Secretary Thouvenel took leave of the Emperor.

TALKING IN THE HILLS

November 1861

Juan Antonio went for a walk with friends Garcia and Diego. Despite the fact that the Mexican states were blessed with ample sunlight San Luis Potosí was at a very high elevation and the winters were severe. Already the temperature was quite chilly. The clear winter sun highlighted the brown foothills and mountains against the cloudless azure sky and as the boys started to climb the brush became increasingly sparse. From this altitude the boys could gaze down upon San Luis and behold it in its entirety. This was a favorite activity of theirs; Juan had also wanted to join them but had to work making saddles. When they had climbed to their old spot with the "sitting rocks" they sat down.

The three friends all wore ponchos against the chill and were wearing their sombreros for warmth, and shade, as well. They were all armed against wild animals or banditos – Juan Antonio with his father's revolver rifle, Garcia with a pistol and all three carried hiltless cutting knives.

"Do you think the Europeans will actually invade?" Garcia asked.

Diego replied "I think they are just trying to get their money from us. We buy their merchandise, and there are still many Spaniards here with haciendas. Think of all the printing presses, porcelain, clocks, train parts and other goods we buy from them. They won't actually invade us – just oblige us to repay their loans."

"Well I don't know." Juan Antonio said. "My father says Presidente Juárez is really worried and Ponciano Arriaga is always in México City nowadays. He says the Europeans have inflated the figures owed to them and are demanding very high interest rates, especially the French. I think they can always depend on someone else to buy their machinery or porcelain."

The boys paused for a minute to admire the view of their city. From up here it all seemed so simple; the beautiful Cathedral with the Palacio del Gobierno and the Plaza de Armas in front of it, the gardens of the Templo del Carmen, Iglesia de San Francisco and the Plaza de San Francisco on the south. They could identify the post and telegraph office, the dry goods stores, the market and the stables for passing coaches. From the center of town the stone and wood houses extended outward. They stared down on their fellow townspeople and observed the rituals of daily life continuing as if there were no menace.

"What does your father say about the norteamericanos?" Garcia asked; standing to stretch his legs and crossing his arms.

"He says Juárez is working to settle separately with them." Juan Antonio replied. "They aren't threatening military intervention but – and this is totally secret so you must swear not to tell anyone else – agreed? The norteamericanos are asking for a reduced interest rate with a six-year payback period. But as collateral they want Baja California, Chihuahua, Sonora and Sinaloa!"

"Dios!" Garcia said. "They always want our land! We cannot stop them! First Tejas, then Alta California and Nuevo México, now the northwest quarter of our country! It's the same demand they made eight years ago to Santa Anna and he sold them more of our territory! And they are the ones who ended up with all the Californian gold! Now the Europeans want us to pay them and bleed us!"

Garcia drew a breath.

"The French are doing the same thing they did in 1838 for the Guerra de los Pasteles – when they exaggerated the debt from the Tejas war and the French pastry company! Their navy bombarded and seized Veracruz and took out customs receipts for seven months! Then England stepped in and charged us for them to 'persuade' the French to accept our paying only their initial demands for our money and not more! I tell you, be it land or be it money – they always want something!"

"And think if we still had Alta California and the gold there?" Diego said. "And the Europeans? What right do France, England and Spain have to tell us what to do? I like Spain and my family is of Spanish heritage but I won't stand for their troops on our land ever again! Juárez is right, I say 'No intervención!'".

Diego had become animated during his speech and stood up next to Garcia. Now only Juan Antonio remained seated. "You're right," he said. "My father was in Zacatecas last week and he said he spoke with General Ortega about the situation. Presidente Juárez won't let the Europeans hold Veracruz like they did last time. If they attack, Ortega is certain there will be a general conscription. My father says we can all serve under General Ortega!"

With this statement, Juan Antonio lifted himself from the rock, leveled his rifle at a rock approximately eighty yards away and fired. Fine white dust kicked up from where the bullet ricocheted off the rock.

"I say if the Europeans invade, we'll be ready!"

ENTER THE EUROPEANS

December 1861– January 1862

On the morning of December 8th, 1861 Spanish marines and dragoons garrisoned in Cuba embarked for the port of Veracruz. They reached it on the tenth and had occupied the city by the 17th, disembarking under the watchful eyes of their naval gunners.

The Mexican garrison leaders in the fort of San Juan de Ulúa knew they could not possibly succeed at repelling the Spanish alone, much less the Triumvirate alliance and they had been given orders to avoid conflict at all costs. The Mexican soldiers withdrew from the city, but not before dismantling or spiking all of their cannons, herding the cattle out of the city, and issuing instructions that anyone supplying or giving shelter to any of the Europeans would be punished as a traitor.

The citizens of Veracruz barricaded every street to inhibit cavalry and artillery movements and barred themselves in their homes or abandoned the city. Consequently; the Spanish expeditionary force of sixty-two hundred soldiers was forced to supply itself by ocean from Cuba.

By the beginning of the new year, the Mexican soldiers had distributed themselves in a loose screen across the villages west of Veracruz, and in the city of Puebla inland, on the road to the capital. These soldiers were ill prepared for battle; most lacked uniforms, only one out of every three or four had a rifle, and the ones that did have were decades old; and the rest carried field machetes or knives. There they sat and waited while the pieces were moved into place on the chessboard.

Presidente Benito Juárez, authorized by the Congreso to conduct negotiations, dispatched General Ignacio Zaragoza to the city of Puebla to organize the defense of México, and General Manuel Doblado to Veracruz to attempt to negotiate terms with the Spanish, who had been joined on January 6th, 1862 by eight hundred British marines and on January 8th by three thousand French marines.

General Doblado was instructed to obtain settlement, if at all possible, but if an agreement could not be reached, then at least he could buy México precious time to prepare itself.

LA SOLEDAD

January 10, 1862

"Señor Presidente, the telegram from General Doblado has come in."

Benito Pablo Juárez Garcia looked up from his desk and took the folded telegram from his assistant. His complexion was darker than most due to his Zapotecan Indian heritage. He had a broad, chiseled nose and narrow eyebrows which conveyed a grave countenance to most. Those who knew him spoke ceaselessly of his gravity, honesty and dedication. For Benito Juárez nothing came before his devotion to México. In all his years as the leader of México, he had striven to guide México through one crisis after another.

There appeared to be no end to the problems. He had endured war and exile, had been besieged and imprisoned, and had almost been murdered unceremoniously in a prison cell in Guadalajara. Some of his closest friends had laid down their lives so that México might be free – free from the Spanish, free from Santa Anna, free from the Conservatives. And now, it appeared more would die by

European hands. Already fifty-five, Juárez felt his age and wondered if he would outlive the European menace.

As he opened the telegram the Presidente told himself he had not had a choice on the moratorium; México could not continue paying her debts at this point. The interest payments alone were suffocating the country and restructuring was unavoidable. The telegram read as follows:

La Soledad
January 10, 1862
Señor Presidente,

They accepted the preliminaries, Negotiating with Sr. Charles Wyke of England, Sr. Juan Prim of Spain and Sr. Dubois de Saligny of France, Declare no hostile intent but demand satisfaction of debt or hostilities will erupt, Will attempt to reduce amounts and delay.

General Doblado
Secretary of Foreign Relations

Juárez doubted it would be possible to negotiate with the Europeans. While they might not actually invade, they were certain to use force to extort more financial concessions from México.

Above all, he needed time – time for General Zaragoza to train his soldiers and fortify the garrison protecting Puebla. The more time passed, the more painful the European occupation would be for the Europeans and the better prepared the Mexican army would be. They could not accept any increase in the amounts because what was already being claimed was well beyond what the country could bear. México had no room for negotiation and could not afford a war. His head swam from the plots hidden inside of plots, the danger that was coalescing as he sat there thinking. What did each of the European powers want? Could he recognize it in time to avoid a trap?

Prior to the start of the American civil war, Juárez would have played the Europeans off of the Americans. He was certain that Abraham Lincoln knew the subjugation of México by Europe was a means to an end – that the plan within the plan was to create a satellite nation subservient to European interests in the Western Hemisphere. England and France traded openly with the secessionist southern states and any fool could see that the Europeans were trying to apply the principle of divide and conquer on their rising competitor. There was even talk of the reinstitution of slavery in México! May God never let it come to that! So quickly could their gains of previous decades be erased by European guns.

Guns, guns, guns. Juárez knew his army was woefully lacking in them. Most of the soldiers who were heroically prepared to lay down their lives could not even have the dignity of doing so properly armed and outfitted. And Abraham Lincoln, who several months ago had agreed to a loan of nine million dollars to assist in México's debt restructuring, had subsequently changed his mind. Now the Americans would not even sell the Mexican government arms or materiel for fear of upsetting the Europeans. He had received their final answer in the negative hardly nine days ago. This was the one time when the Monroe Doctrine would have benefited México but the United States was not in a position to enforce it.

Juárez rubbed his forehead to assuage the headache and tension he felt. These were certainly desperate times and he was resolved to adopt severe measures. A sweeping conscription of any male fit to bear arms, from the youngest to the oldest, and the death penalty without exception to those who aided the enemy. Should the Europeans appear to want more than just their money, then truly every Mexican citizen would be needed. This could be México's darkest hour. Would she survive?

JUAN'S DEPARTURE

February 1862

It was a cold winter day and Juan Antonio, Diego, Garcia and Juan were walking along the streets of San Luis Potosí. A strong bitter wind swept down from the hills and the boys crossed their arms under their woolen ponchos to stay warm. Juan had chosen to volunteer for the Mexican army, and as a volunteer he could choose where he enlisted and was traveling to Querétaro to sign up with his elder cousin so they could be in the same unit. Although there were no open hostilities, people did not expect the ongoing negotiations Doblado undertook in La Soledad to convince the Europeans to leave in peace.

Matters had grown very serious in their country. The Mexican government had allowed the European forces to lodge themselves in three towns away from the tropical coast where the humidity and mosquitoes depleted them but outside of these towns, all contact with the Europeans was regarded as treason and was a capital offense.

Presidente Juárez had publicly issued a six-point resolution to both the Mexican people and the Europeans that had been posted in every town in México. These points asserted that México was capable of resolving her own problems; that México would be governed by a representative government and not by an occupying power; that foreign occupation was illegal; that, should negotiations fail, the Mexican army would defend México; that hospitals housing sick or wounded foreigners would forfeit these persons as prisoners of war, and that the original disembarkation in Veracruz would be treated as an invasion. Should negotiations fail, México would defend herself to the death, fighting the invaders in every pueblo, arroyo and mountain pass across the country.

Everyone felt that war would soon break out and a broad general draft would follow. Juan had discussed the impending conflict with his family. They thought that, since Juan and his cousin were at the age when they would be among the first to be called to arms and sent to fight, it was best for the boys to enlist together instead of ending up in different units.

The four Potosíno boys were pensive as they walked slowly toward the stagecoach stop. Juan carried an old cap-and-ball percussion revolver with him. He would have to acquire a rifle in the field. Juan's friends were sad to see their friend of many years go, and the weight of what the future held for them pressed heavily upon them. In contrast, they envied him for taking the steps toward achieving manhood that they had not yet taken.

Although it was late afternoon, the streets were quiet due to the chilly mountain wind and the national crisis. The bright winter sun forced them to squint, and the solemnity of the moment inhibited conversation. Before the gravity of Juan's departure, all topics seemed trivial. Nevertheless, they talked to keep their spirits up.

As they rounded the corner and walked into the plaza the stagecoach was preparing to leave. It was a simple coach; its black paint had a thick layer of dust and was chipped, but the large rear wheels looked solidly braced, and it did not appear as if it would bounce and jostle the passengers too much. The interior lacked upholstery, and the doors were thin for its body, the panels barely half an inch thick.

The coach was already full, as was the luggage space on the roof, so the driver asked Juan to sit with him on the driver's board in the front. Juan placed his sack in the foot space of the coach interior and turned to say goodbye to his childhood friends.

"Well, this is it." he said reluctantly.

"Yes." Diego said. "Write us a letter if you can. Let us know. Mail me and I'll tell everybody."

"I will. I'm certain I'll have the time. My cousin and I will probably end up waiting around in Puebla. If you go there, look for me in the Querétaro regiment."

"No problem, we'll do it." The boys all nodded emphatically and looked intensely at Juan.

With that Juan turned, took the driver's hand, and climbed up to the driving board. Other passengers were still saying their farewells through the window or were talking with their relatives through the open doors. The three friends stood by the coach awkwardly, kicking the dirt and waving weakly. Eventually the other passengers completed saying "Adios", and the driver snapped the reins, and the horses pulled forward. Juan turned around, grabbing the roof rail, and waved good-bye to his lifetime friends, who waved back.

The homes of San Luis Potosí moved past the coach as it headed through the town to the south. As they hit the outskirts the driver turned to Juan and struck up a conversation.

"You got a pistol?"

"Yes. Won't shoot very far but it's still good."

"You can help defend us if we get attacked by banditos. Anybody comes out from behind rocks or on a horse with a gun, you just shoot them. I've got my shotgun here under my feet but I'll have to race the horses if we get held up."

"Sure. I'll do it. I just don't know if that will help me if they have rifles."

"Well, usually they get close enough, but if there's too many, just let it go and drop it so they can see it. Sometimes they don't want to kill you."

"That's good. I don't want to die before my time."

"Boy, when you die that's your time. When you're an old man like me you'll see it that way. But I don't want to scare you, there shouldn't be any problem. It's not a long journey and there aren't any tight passes. Are you heading to Puebla to fight?"

"If that is God's will, yes, I'm going to fight."

"So are you going straight there? Your ticket is only to Querétaro."

"I'm stopping at Querétaro to enlist with my cousin. They're calling for volunteers there and I wanted to be together with him."

"That's a good idea. You're a buen muchacho! I'm proud to have you in my coach! It wouldn't surprise me to see them attack us again. Spain thinks we still belong to them, and who knows what the French and the English want. We will never be free from them without beating them, be it the gringos or the gabachos. They'll only leave us alone if we fight it out with them."

"You're right."

"It's different this time you know. Actually, it's not different, it's just now we are free to fight. With the yanquis and the gabachos, Santa Anna kept having us fight and then he would sell us out for money. He kept all the money that the norteamericanos paid him from the Guadalupe Hidalgo and Gadsen treaties, you know."

"I guess he kept a lot of it."

"No, he kept all of it. The people, us, our lands, were nothing to him. He was the worst thing that could have happened to us. We'd fight, lose, fight, and lose again. Every time there was a rebellion, he'd take European loans to buy off his enemies and we'd be in more debt. But this time it will be different. Everyone knows we're fighting for ourselves, not for Santa Anna. They won't walk over us this time! I'll go fight myself."

"Yes. We'll probably have to fight."

"You just remember. Those gabachos have cannons and rifles and horses. But they still bleed. You just have to get close to them."

"At Puebla I imagine General Zaragoza will have us defend from cover and make them charge us. Then it will be one-on-one. I'm sure I'll stand and not flee."

"Yes, it's better to die fighting. You know, if you turn and run, they'll shoot you in the back."

"I will never run." Juan said, his voice trailing off.

The driver agreed that conflict was the only option and continued to pontificate on the expected war between the Europeans and México. The coach traveled through the foothills to the south, and when the coach would crest a rise Juan could see far across the landscape. The land was arid and brown for as far as he could see, broken by ridges of rock and short bushes somehow drawing life from the dry soil.

This was their land, their México, and the driver was right – after decades of leadership that exploited her, México was ready to defend herself. The Europeans would never break her spirit. But how many would die before they realized this?

THE UNION FLAG

March 1862

It was afternoon and Captain Sharpe, Royal Marine, sat at a small collapsible wooden table in a spartan hut that he shared with another English marine captain. Officers bivouacked in the Mexican highland villages west of Veracruz were usually fortunate enough to be lodged in a farmer's hut and not in a tent outdoors, and there were times when the breeze blew away some of the humidity and odor.

The hut's interior walls bore a simple whitewash splash that was years old and quite dirty. The original inhabitants' cookware still hung from hooks on the wall. The Mexicans had abandoned their houses before the English arrived, and one never saw them because they were prohibited from contact with the Triple Alliance's forces. Veracruz and the surrounding area had become occupied ghost towns.

They had been languishing there two months and had accomplished nothing except losing men daily to the scourges of yellow fever and diarrhea. Of course, Captain Sharpe knew his duty was to serve England, regardless of circumstance, but he did wish that the haggling at La Soledad would cease and they would get their money or conquer Mexico. At least conditions were more reasonable away from the Gulf of Mexico coastline.

It was not easy staying in Mexico. The diet was rough on their systems; only beans and tortillas to eat – what he wouldn't do for a shepherd's pie or some porridge! The humidity never broke; and starting even when they arrived in early January the men had begun to fall sick. Life for the remaining fit and healthy settled into the dreary routine of drilling and mustering to arms.

Now Sharpe was studying an outdated issue of the American journal *Harper's Weekly* that he had bartered for with a French marine from the adjacent village. In it was an illustration of the feared Confederate ironclad, the *CSS Virginia* referred to by its original name, the *Merrimack*. Those Yanks sure had audacity! Scuttled by the withdrawing northern forces in Norfolk, the ironclad *Merrimack* had been rebuilt by the southerners as the *Virginia* and it was a monster! A couple of weeks back the *Virginia* had engaged – and sunk – some of the finest Federal frigates at sea, right under the guns of the naval batteries in Maryland! The French marine who had traded him the magazine to him had heard an eyewitness account secondhand. The Confederates had waxed the ironsides with tallow so that even the balls from the shore batteries would be deflected off the hull! The next day the same *Virginia* had engaged the *USS Monitor* point-blank and the two behemoths had fired at one another the whole day.

If this continued, and the Confederacy continued to boost its navy with frigates and ironclads built in England, they might beat the Union blockade and its Navy!

Officially, Britain had many months previously issued a Proclamation of Neutrality reinforcing the provisions of the Foreign Enlistment Act. This act outlawed British citizens from fighting for one side or the other as well as prohibited the sale of warships to either side. But, southern cotton exported from Matamoros in the north of Mexico was highly valued in England, and the Confederates were not driving very hard bargains to purchase British manufactured goods and arms.

And, the effrontery of the North, first in boarding the *HMS Trent* and seizing the Confederate envoys in November and then the attempt to surreptitiously sail out of England with all its saltpeter! Thank heavens Parliament had declared a total embargo on arms to America otherwise they wouldn't have had any gunpowder!

The trick for England would have to be to let the North and the South beat one another to death. Britain could still sell ships to the Confederacy – of course, under present legislation these ships had to sail unnamed from the shores of England until they arrived in the Bahamas, where they would be armed. British captains were making a fortune by running merchandise through the Union blockade from the Caribbean.

When the North was weak enough, there was a force of eight thousand soldiers in Quebec, sent there a few months back, who could invade and enter on the side of the Confederacy, and avenge the disgrace of the *Trent* affair. It would then be a simple matter for the eight hundred marines in Veracruz to sail north and take Washington by storm. Billy Yank would have a hard time indeed! And Her Majesty's navy could assist the Confederate navy... already the Union was feeling the pinch as was evidenced by their issue of a new green paper currency, the so-called "greenbacks", to fund the war effort.

Sharpe reconsidered.

Well, that was probably going a tad too far. The arms embargo had been lifted, and Union ships had avoided confrontation with Her Majesty's navy – even when provoked. And even though they were wounded, the Yanks would still bite back; they had learned that in '12.

Captain Sharpe was interrupted from his daydream by the bugler sounding an officer's muster. Tossing the *Harper's Weekly* down on the table, he leaped up from his chair, put on his red officer's coat over his white shirt, quickly polished the buttons on the front of his coat and on his cuffs and grabbed his black officer's hat. In the humidity even the hat seemed limp and its sides drooped.

He walked briskly out of the hut and down the street toward the center of the village, where the church was, two streets away. White buildings, brown tile or thatch roofs, and humidity, bloody humidity! Enough to make a chap go balmy!

Marines loitered about bare-chested, idly making chat or playing cards. A few of them almost forgot to salute him as he passed; he would discuss this with the provosts. The wait was sapping their morale.

As he reached the church the sentry on duty, already at attention, said "G'day sir." At least this gentleman was wearing his blue coat and held his Enfield rifle as if he intended to use it one day. The union flag fluttered over the door.

Entering through the narrow wooden double doors, Sharpe saw he was one of the last to arrive. The others were making small talk and he sat in one of the rear pews next to a young leftenant named Godsbury.

In front of the approximately two dozen assembled officers was a map of North America on a wooden two-legged stand. It was unmarked, but even from four rows back Sharpe could see it was faded and worn from the constant shifting of pieces over it, tracking military movements.

Sharpe was barely settled in when the orderly arrived and, stomping his heel, cried out "Attention!"

The officers rose to their feet in unison and turned to the rear of the building from where the Colonel entered. *Standard field briefing.*

"Stand down." the Colonel ordered flatly, walking to the side of the map.

"Right. Now, I'm sure by now all of you are privy to the arrival of the contingent of French forces a week ago. The force is much larger than their initial expeditionary force and brings their entire number to ninety-six hundred – superior in quantity to us and the Spanish combined. This excludes their incapacitated and casualties from yellow fever. They are under the command of General Lorencez and have already been barracked in Veracruz and its environs.

"We cannot as yet ascertain Napoléon's true intent but methinks he intends to follow in the footsteps of his uncle. As you know, our lines of communication are slowed by the continued inoperability of the transatlantic cable. Thus, our special envoy, Sir Charles Wyke, still awaits a return from Lord Palmerston and Her Majesty Queen Victoria. Moreover, we remain engaged in diplomatic parleys at La Soledad with that blasted ditherer, Doblado. Once we have a reply from England, which we hope to receive most expeditiously, we will see if our diplomatic posture has changed.

"If the French intend to colonize Mexico, we could well have another Waterloo on our hands, but I'm sure with our Spanish allies the result would be the same. However, until such time that we have a reply from Parliament our mission remains unchanged – to assure the prompt repayment of Mexico's financial obligations to England, with proper and due interest. No more; no less.

"In so far as the sacking of the British Legation the sixteenth of November, 1860 and the theft of one hundred fifty thousand pounds sterling, as well as the murder of seventy-three of Her Majesty's subjects – souls shot in a ditch at Tacubaya – it would seem diplomacy is the mood of the day. Comeuppance shall have to wait; our superiors aren't of mind to take umbrage at this present time.

"Lastly, I'm aware that some of you entertain rumours concerning attacks against the Yanks. The official position of Her Majesty is one of neutrality. Now, should the Americans have the cheek to back their Monroe Doctrine with powder and shot, why then we'll have a go at them! As to French and Spanish intentions, if Madrid wants their old colony back, it would appear they will have to go through the French now.

"My personal view is that the best thing to happen would be for some Yankee bank in the United States to lend the Mexicans the money to pay us, but I rather doubt that will occur.

"Right. Very good then lads. God save the Queen! Dismissed."

Formally excused, Captain Sharpe lifted his hat, and wiped the sweat from his brow. Bloody French; what he wouldn't do to have at them! Those French spent all their time looking at themselves in the mirror and not at the enemy! Turning to Godsbury, he said "Oy – Geoff. How about those French? Always looking to have a go aren't they?"

"You said it. Mind you, I reckon we should have never teamed up with them. No good will come of this."

"No good indeed."

The men had stood, and were returning to the heat and humidity of the tropical Mexican sun.

"Cor, 'otter than an oven here, I tell you." said Godsbury.

"Yes. You hear about that Yankee naval battle near Washington?" Sharpe asked.

"Yes. I hope they got photographs of that one! First time you get real photos of battles, it is! They say the South is asking us to make them ironclads. I get out of the service, first thing I'm doing is running guns to the Johnny Rebs! Put the Union flag on any old sloop, sail to the Bahamas with yer hold chock-full of guns, mirrors, clocks and perfumes; get a Southerner to sail you past the blockade and offload the booty in the South – or even Matamoros if you're scared of the Union boys. They make a killing!"

"If the Yankees and the Rebs keep at it, you'll get your shot, I say! Shall we have a pint then?"

"Yep, let's drink one to the French and their attempt to recolonize the Americas! Let the bloody Yanks whistle Yankee Doodle Dandee out their arses!"

Laughing the soldiers entered the tavern to drink grog and pass away the afternoon.

MÉXICO CITY

April 12, 1862

It was morning and Juan Antonio was with his father in México City. They were staying with friends of his mother who lived there and had opened their home to them. His father had brought him here because he wanted to meet with General Ortega, as well as be closer to the action. It was Juan Antonio's first time in the capital and he had been overwhelmed when they arrived by coach yesterday. Many of the buildings had three, sometimes four, stories! And the streets were so wide three buggies could pass abreast.

Horses, carts, and carriages passed through the streets, kicking up dust incessantly and requiring one to be constantly on guard once beyond the hitching-post line. And what hitching-posts they had! Some were made of embellished metal, not like the simple wooden logs nailed together in San Luis Potosí! All of the merchants' buildings had big signs; DRY GOODS, TAILORS, BUTCHER, WAREHOUSE, APOTHECARY... Also, everyone seemed in a hurry; they did not amble and greet each other openly like in the mountains.

And, it was so big! He estimated that he could walk for half an hour and not hit a farm. Of course, there were the plazas and the homes where horses weren't stabled or kept in fenced yards, but this was truly a grand city.

Now, his father was reading *El Republicano*, and Juan Antonio, eager to see what was happening, went to the kitchen and got the coffeepot. The cupboards were beautiful, multihued like the house exteriors in the city and the pottery bore Aztec designs. What utensils were not of clay, were of polished brass. Such opulence these city folks displayed.

As he stood over his father's shoulder to pour the coffee, Juan Antonio saw the bold black headlines. Presidente Juárez was going to deliver a speech today from the Palacio Nacional. "DECLARATION OF WAR EXPECTED" stated one bold subtitle; "CALL TO ARMS" read another.

"Call to arms". This was it. This would be why his father wanted to meet with General Ortega this evening. His father would be able to arrange personal service for him under the general, and Juan Antonio would be able to fight in the big war against the world's finest armies!

Reading the small print was fatiguing, so Juan Antonio took a seat again and recommenced eating his breakfast of eggs and beans on a tortilla with hot sauce.

After they had completed their breakfast the two men washed their dishes and walked out into the street, squinting as the sun hit their eyes. The weather was much warmer here in the valley than in the mountains of San Luis Potosí and within a few weeks it would start to turn seriously hot. His father had left his sombrero in San Luis Potosí and was using his smaller gentleman's hat with the narrow brim. Juan Antonio did not have a city hat, as his father referred to it as, but this didn't bother him. They were going to the massive market in the Plaza de la Constitución. There they would buy vegetables and chilies and perhaps some fabric before hearing the presidente speak.

As they walked through the busy streets his father related to him what was going on. General Doblado had stalled the Europeans and pretty much gotten the Spanish and the English to accept a reduced, staggered debt repayment plan. At first the Spanish had been extremely demanding in asking for the recognition of the Mon-Almonte Treaty to compensate Spanish citizens for damages inflicted on them in prior years as well as an obsequious apology from the Mexican government for its previous "so-called misconduct" and the immediate surrender of any port within twenty-four hours of Spanish request. The Mexicans were able to deflect the Spanish demands, and it looked as if after months spent cooling their heels in the foothills, the English and the Spanish would be leaving.

One of the main reasons these countries were desisting was that the French had sent reinforcements and were expected to invade. The French force was small, but their army was one of the world's best. This was a critical time for México. A general conscription would be called nationwide and Juan Antonio would have to fight.

Any hope of an alliance with the other American nations was hopeless because the norteamericanos were embroiled in their civil war and their Central American and Caribbean neighbors could do nothing before the might of the French. México was alone but at least she was not burdened with the yoke of a dictator anymore. Additionally, the past three months had served to deteriorate the European forces and allow the poorly prepared Mexican army time to train.

As Juan Antonio and his father neared the Plaza de la Constitución, the noise of the vendors' cries increased to where they could discern individual voices over the din of the carriages and horses trotting by. The stalls had been pushed to one side of the square, and they were entering on the side of the stalls. The vendors who had not been moved had to compete with those who had shifted from the other side.

Already, a small crowd had gathered in front of the Palacio Nacional and more were entering every minute. While his father shopped, Juan Antonio admired the view of the Palacio Nacional and the Cathedral to his left. The palace was enormous; Juan Antonio counted no less than three dozen identical arched windows on the second story. Most were shuttered so the crowd could not see inside, and they were protected by duplicate small-railed balconies.

Alternating between the balconies were half as many windows on the street level, all arched and shuttered. On the third story were perhaps fifty smaller windows rounded at the top. The parapet roof was decorated by maybe four-dozen matching carved urns, and there were three similar entry façades in addition to tower façades at the corners. From the second window above the central façade a large flag was draped over the unshuttered window and a pair of flags hung from either corner of the balcony. Obviously the Presidente would address the audience from there.

Seeing the eagle framed by the green and red of their national flag swelled him with pride. His thoughts wandered to Juan; surely he was in Puebla by now.

Peering over the crowd and to the left, Juan Antonio could see the Cathedral and its adjoining sacristy; never before had he beheld such a sight! The sacristy's façade was inset with niches and perhaps a dozen statuettes of saints over the door and also along the sides. The Cathedral was framed by twin bell towers. Both structures towered over the sprawling Palacio Nacional, whose breadth spanned the whole plaza.

Scanning for his father he saw him negotiating with a vegetable vendor. Walking over to him, Juan Antonio tapped him on the arm and they walked over to take a place among the crowd to wait.

After at least an hour of standing in place in the plaza waiting while the crowd thickened, the Cathedral's bells began to toll. They tolled in a crescendo, then tolled three times in unison, then stopped.

As the echo carried over the plaza, Presidente Juárez stepped from behind the flag onto the center balcony while six soldiers formed a semi-circle on the plaza, beneath the balcony in front of the portal. It was then Juan Antonio perceived that more soldiers had taken position along the sides of the palace and in front of it.

Juárez was dressed in a black suit and held a rolled piece of paper in his left hand. The multitude fell silent in anticipation of what he was about to say and he raised his right hand before him to greet the assembled citizens.

"Fellow patriots of México, it is with the deepest seriousness I speak to you now. Our negotiation process with the French has failed, and we expect them to attack us any day. While we continue to negotiate with the English and the Spanish, we expect these two nations to withdraw their hostile forces very soon. However, even through protracted discussion with the French representatives, we could not reach an agreement. Indeed, the French have insulted our national dignity by refusing to recognize our government as the representative government of México."

With this statement murmurs of discontent and anger swept through the group and the Presidente raised his right hand in a gesture requesting silence while lowering his gaze to read the paper in his left hand.

"As such, we declare the troops of France to be invaders of our country, and the Congreso has declared war upon France. We have also issued the following edicts which are effective immediately:

"First, any Frenchman committing violence will be duly punished and collaborators tried as traitors with complete property forfeiture,

"Second, all male citizens aged twenty to sixty will be conscripted, evaders shall be prosecuted as traitors,

"Third, state governments are hereby authorized to raise troops locally,

"Fourth, state governments are authorized to use any available resource in defense of our soil,

"Fifth, French nationals residing in our country shall be subject to national law,

"Finally, anyone aiding the French shall be executed."

Juan Antonio's mind raced with the gravity of the situation. Although he himself was not going to be drafted, his father would be, most certainly marching off with a Potosíno regiment in the near future. There was no way he could let his father serve alone!

Juárez spoke again.

"These are trying times for our cherished nation and once again we are all asked to put aside our political differences in the greater interest of the Mexican nation. I call upon all of you, Conservatives, Constitutionalists, patriots of our homeland, to unite under the same flag to repel the invaders! Should we fail, our land will revert to being a European colony again, after we struggled so hard to cast off the yoke of three centuries of repression by Spain!"

Juan Antonio's hand lifted to the right side of his face, his fingers touching lightly in a posture of thought. Certainly if he volunteered to serve for General Ortega, he would not be able to remain with his father, as General Ortega was from Zacatecas and would have those people under his personal command. Should either of them fall… Juan Antonio dared not think further.

Presidente Juárez appeared to be concluding.

"Compatriots, understand your sacred duty to yourselves, your families and your nation. Conscriptions will begin in the next few days and will continue until every last foreigner is driven from our soil. May God protect us all."

With that, the Presidente turned and left the balcony. The crowd was dead silent for an instant, then everyone began to speak with their colleagues so that the marketplace was abuzz with the animated babble of anxious men.

Juan Antonio turned to his father and their eyes met.

"You see." his father said "I told you that soon enough you would have a chance to fight."

As Juan Antonio looked at his father he noticed the wrinkles around his eyes. His father suddenly seemed very tired. Juan Antonio had never thought of his father as tired, or even old for that matter. And for the first time he realized rather poignantly that his father was mortal. Feeling a wave of empathy for his father, he said "Father, we can enlist together."

"Now, now. Let's not discuss this here. Let's wait and see what Jesús Ortega says. Remember that we're meeting him for a tequila tonight?

"All right, I remember. But I don't see why we can't discuss it now."

Putting his arm around his son, Juan Antonio's father said "Let's not spoil a beautiful day. We shan't have too many together for some time. Let's drop off the vegetables and stroll around the city. People will be in a talkative mood today, that's for sure."

And so the two shuffled out of the plaza with the crowd, not saying another word.

TEQUILA WITH ORTEGA

April 12, 1862

Juan Antonio and his father spent the afternoon and early evening walking the streets and chatting with the townspeople. In general folks were nervous but also determined; there was a sense México had come of age and would no longer tolerate being pushed around. When the hour came of their appointment with General Ortega came, they went to the saloon near the Alameda park. They could hear the loud conversation drifting out into the evening sky even as they walked past the hitching posts, stepped onto the porch, and pushed through the swinging half-doors.

The saloon was full and most of the clientele seemed to be locals; their dress was formal and they were not rough around the edges. Men wore town hats, not sombreros and no weapons or lace-adorned women were in sight.

They spotted Ortega at the bar just as he noticed them. He motioned them over to the bar. He was a grave man, bearing a serious expression on his face, accentuated by his dark, sloping eyebrows and stiff posture.

"Francisco" said Ortega, warmly shaking Juan Antonio's father's hand.

"Jesús. Good to see you!" his father, Francisco Ayala, replied.

"Buenas noches, Señor Ortega!" said Juan Antonio, shaking the General's hand.

"Come. Let's sit and have a drink."

They made their way over to a small table. Ortega signaled for a bottle of tequila to be brought over.

Juan Antonio's father spoke first. "Well, it will be war then."

"Yes, but it was always going to go that way. Doblado tried valiantly to persuade them to leave in peace but the French were not going to be swayed. Their demands for money are just a front for their true intent of taking us over."

"Are the norteamericanos going to give us any money?"

"No, unfortunately not. The only thing they're doing is restructuring the debt from six percent to three percent interest. They won't sell us arms or uniforms either; they're nervous about taking sides for the time being."

"That's bad, we needed that." replied Juan Antonio's father, pausing to pour tequila in everyone's shot glass.

"I propose a toast." Ortega announced. "To the ardent defense of our homeland! May God bring us victory." With that the three men raised their shot glasses and took a drink.

"So what's your plan, then?" inquired his father as they sat down.

"I'm to serve although I'm not sure yet in what capacity. They keep wanting me to be a supply master or a bureaucratic general instead of one fighting in the field. You know, no matter how many victories I win, they will never overlook my lack of military training."

"I'm sure they'll give you a big army, General Ortega." Juan Antonio interjected.

"So then, if it were your decision Congreso would give me an army big enough to invade France, right?"

The trio laughed and then Juan Antonio's father spoke politely. "Juan Antonio is, as previously discussed, interested in serving under your command, Jesús."

"Is that so, mi amigo? I know you're experienced and you can read and write. That already makes you more qualified than half my junior officers! It would be my honor to have you serving under me. I'd already said as much to your father. Your patriotism runs deep."

"But General Ortega, would it be possible for my father and me to serve together – as father and son?"

"Now that I don't know... I can only arrange for young volunteers under my wing." stated the General, glancing sidelong at Francisco.

"Hey, Jesús doesn't need an old man like me around." said Juan Antonio's father. "Besides, my place is with the Potosinos. We all know one another, and I could never serve with another town's regiment, especially at my age. You are young and brave and we both know you'll do us proud. You have a destiny to fulfill and as for me, I've had my time. My place is with my town."

"But Father, you'll just be a regular soldier with the Potosíno regiment." Juan Antonio protested.

"Do I deserve better?" Francisco asked. "I'm an older man and I've never fought. It has to be this way. I will be fine. Now come, the matter is settled; let's not dampen General Ortega's evening with this gloomy talk. He has a war to fight." Francisco lifted his tequila glass and shifted his eyes away from his son.

General Ortega glanced over at Juan Antonio and said "What we'll do is this; I'll send a telegraph for you when I have my own command. Your father will be conscripted well before you and we already decided to handle it this way. You wouldn't want to waste your time camping out and sharing a tent would you?"

Juan Antonio nodded without replying. It would be pointless to argue now as his father and Ortega had clearly prearranged all of this.

The men spent the evening discussing the negotiations at La Soledad, the poor state of readiness of the Mexican army and their lack of weapons, and predictions of which cities would suffer attacks. When it got late, Ortega excused himself and they all left the saloon together. On the way home, Juan Antonio kept glancing at the beautiful clear spring evening sky filled with stars. Despite the implications of the day's events, he felt elated. He was going to fight!

ACQUIESCENCE FROM THE SMOKY PARLOR

April 1862

Across the Atlantic, in one of the most opulent parlors London's privileged could afford, three Englishmen were seated conversing. Their chairs were set in a rough circle, but, owing to the dim illumination in the room, their faces were indistinguishable.

Everything in the room displayed social rank and ostentation: snifters of the finest French cognac, high-backed chairs with plush buttoned padding, top hats of the highest quality resting on beautiful hat stands, and velvet curtains screening the windows of their private room.

The smoke from their cigars filled the room, and what little light penetrated the interior came as refracted beams diffused by the thick tobacco smoke. These were important men in British society who wished to meet in secrecy and this dark secluded smoking room served this purpose for them intermittently.

In the corner, one could just discern the brass handle embedded with a glass centerpiece that opened the back entrance to the room.

Behind that door, three coachmen awaited their masters with their heads down, not speaking. Their coaches were parked separately, several streets away.

"I dare say, they've outplayed us, they have, those French." one of the men in the circle said. "Concluding the London Convention with us all that while. Even Lord Cowley didn't foresee this." he added.

"Indeed." a second man said. "Gun-barrel elections of the former Mexican ambassador, Almonte, while they arranged the installation of that Austrian archduke Maximilian to be a Catholic emperor under their thumb. The gall of it all! Between shielding Rome with their troops and putting a Catholic monarch in Mexico, the French are really up to something."

"Well chaps," the third man said authoritatively, "they've outmaneuvered us and there's not a damn thing we can do about it. It is, quite naturally, humiliating in a way I suppose. But this can be a blessing in disguise. We failed in the United States in twelve, the Spanish failed in Mexico in twenty-nine. Now the French want to have a go. I say let them have it. Godspeed! Britain's best interests are still served and we are saved the dirty work. And we might have gotten involved in another Crimea. Who wants to read stories in the papers like those from Sebastopol?

"There will still be a European buffer state, albeit not an English one, to check the Americans if they succeed, and if they fail they'll bleed themselves trying. Regardless of what transpires, we need to ensure the capital flow to Her Majesty wouldn't you say?

"This said, we'd better make damn sure that Maximilian knows the British butter his bread too! And even Her Majesty, the Queen, can't disagree with me this time; after all, we're helping to support England. She might even compliment me for once!"

The other two men nodded and grunted their assent.

"In the north of the Americas the Yanks are tearing themselves to shreds, and here our popular resentment of them has faded. The expeditionary force in Canada is returning home and Queen

Victoria seeks to mend fences with the Union. And we can get rich off of commerce with both sides, officially or unofficially."

The first man spoke again. "Did you hear the rumour that the French are going to let Santa Anna back into Mexico?"

The other men chuckled and the third said "Yes, just to sow confusion I imagine. Mind you, old de Lopez would be just as good a candidate for emperor as Maximilian, if they'll have him. Just keep him in gold and mistresses for the rest of his days and he'll do whatever you want!"

All the men laughed heartily and puffed on their cigars for a while.

Finally, the third man spoke again. "Right, here's what we'll do then. We'll publicly condemn the French for violating the London Convention. The Spanish will follow suit. I'll take care of the *Times* so that this happens in such a way that in several weeks, when we properly wish the French well, it will not seem undue. But we make it clear beyond a shadow of a doubt that if ever they stop payments to Britain, they'll have the Union Flag to worry about and not just a few paltry Mexican rebels!"

With that he leaned forward to tap the ashes from the tip of his cigar into the ashtray with his wizened hand, and one could just see the aged, calculating face of Prime Minister Palmerston.

THE LETTER

May 4, 1862

It was late in the evening and General Charles Latrille de Lorencez sat in his ornate field tent trying to relax and forget his tension. Outside the tent, in the village of Amozoc on the outskirts of Puebla, a dry wind howled, presaging what the morning would bring. Not far from the French forces were the Mexican soldiers under the command of General Ignacio Zaragoza, dispersed throughout the ring of forts surrounding the city.

He should not feel so restless! There was nothing to fear; half of the Mexicans did not even have shirts, much less a rifle. The artillery would reduce the forts and they would break the circle with shot and bayonet. He must be confident; uncertainty did not befit a general of the rising Second Empire of France.

Besides, the Mexicans were easily brushed aside. There had already been skirmishes en route inland from Veracruz to Puebla: Fortin de las Flores and Cumbres de Acultingo. The Mexicans had been easily displaced in these encounters. Had not Ambassador de

Saligny assured them they would be welcomed as liberators with flowers? Had they not, in the presence of French soldiers as witnesses, confirmed Mssr. Almonte as Regent? There had been no coercion; he had seen the residents of the village declare it for themselves unanimously before the troops.

Yet, there were so many soldiers and they behaved as if they were going to fight. And his force had already fallen to six thousand due to yellow fever and of those only four thousand were not incapacitated by diarrhea. In reality it wasn't enough to take Puebla.

To think along those lines was counterproductive. Tomorrow would determine if they would capture Mexico City; a rapid strike by the infantry against the Guadalupe Hill, overwhelming the defenders before they could concentrate their forces. It was a gamble, but they were ready.

Lorencez lit the second and third candles in the candleholder and glanced around the tent. There, next to his draped field bed, was his leather chest and on top lay his officer's pistol. His saber hung from an adjacent stand, along with his blue jacket embossed with gold buttons and braids, and on top was his peacock style general's hat.

He carried the candleholder over to his collapsible table and picked up the copy of *Les Miserables* by that author Victor Hugo he had been reading in his spare moments. He had been fortunate enough to purchase a copy just before his departure from France in March. It had come out just as they sailed for Mexico and was the talk of Paris. Such a work! One could not sit at a café in Paris without talking about it with your neighbor.

News had also reached him of a popular theater piece *"La Tombee de Mexique"* – *The Fall of Mexico* – that was running in the operas now. It ended with the Tricolore fluttering triumphantly over Mexico City after a bloodless conquest.

Well, he would give his fellow countrymen what they thirsted for by sweeping the Mexicans before him like dust under the broom! Long live the Emperor! Long live the Empire! Vive la France!

65

Rubbing his chin and emboldened by the image of himself delivering Mexico to the Empire, he began to write a letter to the war minister in Paris who would praise his confidence.

4 Mai, 1862

Your Excellency,
Before the Mexicans is a race of such superiority in organization, discipline, morality and intellect that I beg Your Excellency's understanding when I declare that, now, at the head of six thousand soldiers, I am ruler of Mexico!"

General Lorencez continued writing until he was finished, certain of his pending glorious victory and place in history. Tomorrow, the "*cinco de Mayo*" as the locals would say, he would take his place in the annals of the Empire! Folding the letter, he summoned the sentry and ordered it sent as an urgent communiqué. Then he turned in to get some sleep.

Outside the hot wind blew.

EL CINCO DE MAYO

May 5, 1862

By the end of the following day the cactus fields that lay before the eastern forts of Guadalupe and Hidalgo were thick with mud – and French dead. Perhaps five hundred lay either in the mud in front of Lorencez, captured by the Mexicans, or wounded in Amozoc.

The army had already started to withdraw back to Orizaba, their original garrison west of Veracruz. Due to the thick rain Lorencez could not see the enemy in the forts, even with his field glasses, but he was certain they would be celebrating.

The gravity of the situation hung heavily upon him. Undoubtedly his head would roll and he would be replaced for incompetence, just like his predecessor who had permitted the Mexicans to stall. The artillery had not reduced the forts due to the distance and elevation and multiple bayonet charges had not succeeded in overwhelming them. The Mexicans had fought like possessed animals; some only with machetes! Now the French forces were in danger of encirclement by these primitives and needed to withdraw at once.

The Emperor might even find some pretense to imprison him for this. If only he could stop that letter! They would think he had recklessly thrown the men into danger for personal glory. Would they be wrong? Perhaps most of the casualties would turn out to be Zouaves, Arab conscripts, as the Third Zouaves had led most of the assaults. That would diminish the furor back home. Regardless, such a humiliating defeat would not go unpunished.

The already grey sky was darkening fast so Lorencez turned and walked toward his waiting aides-de-camp, his knee-high leather boots sinking in the mud, and his saber banging forgotten against his knee.

VAYAN CON DIOS

May 5, 1862

In the fort of Guadalupe a Mexican soldier was helping to carry the corpses of the fallen back to the wagons. The fighting had been the heaviest here; French cannons had bombarded the ramparts and there had been heavy hand-to-hand combat. Many had died, but, for every Mexican that had fallen, two Frenchmen would not see their homes again! It seemed very sad to carry the fallen comrades from the battlefield, especially after such a great victory. It had taken a long time, and some men were already drinking coffee around a campfire and celebrating loudly.

The body that the soldier was walking to pick up lay with its back to the fort's interior. As he drew closer he recognized it as the young man from Querétaro. Nice boy. It was too bad he had died. Beside him lay the boy's cousin. That's right – they'd enlisted together. At least they died together. *Vayan con Dios.*

Putting Juan's body over his shoulder, the soldier carried him over to the waiting cart. The driver struck up a conversation with him as he approached, and together they lowered Juan down into the cart together.

"Did you hear about the General's message?" the cart driver asked.

"No."

"General Zaragoza sent a message to the Presidente and announced it to us. He said, and I quote, 'The Mexicans arms are covered in glory. The French army attacked with all its might. Its general demonstrated stupidity in the attack.' We are heroes, hermano! Heroes!"

The driver was beaming and slapped the soldier on the back.

The soldier leaned down and patted Juan lightly on the forehead, twice, as a way of saying farewell. He hoped that wherever he was, he had heard Zaragoza's message.

A GLIMMER OF HOPE

May 19, 1862

In México City Presidente Juárez sat in his study, lost in thought. His mood was, as usual, very grave, and his dress austere. He had removed his black jacket and, because he was not anticipating visitors, he loosened his black bow tie and unbuttoned the top button of his shirt so that the upright collar of his white shirt would be less constrictive. He massaged his eyebrows with his left hand and permitted himself an inward sense of optimism, albeit restrained.

The victory at Puebla two weeks past was incontrovertible; the French had withdrawn to Cordoba and Veracruz to lick their wounds and await reinforcements. México had, through her steadfastness, bought precious time to organize and train an army. He had yet to find an answer as to how to fund and equip this army but from all over the country volunteers came by forced march to Puebla and the capital to enlist. Morale was at the highest it had ever been and Puebla had given the people what they needed most; hope and belief that victory was possible. Now it was his responsibility to see that they were able to beat the French.

Running his hands through his wispy hair, he thought how few true leaders his country could depend on. Decades of despotism had created a servile oligarchy that depended upon Santa Anna for its survival. The few men of natural leadership and action who had risen by one means or another during or after Santa Anna's reign had been divided or decimated by the Guerra de la Reforma. He had made every effort to reconcile those leaders of the Conservatives whose intellect he felt could be harnessed to serve their country but, for many, their beliefs were unshakable and in the end they had only betrayed him. He prayed for Melchor Ocampo and Santos Degollado's forgiveness for this. Melchor had been right; most of the former Conservatives could not be trusted and he had paid with his life. Juárez would have to be much more cautious with his amnesties. Melchor had paid for Benito's misplaced trust with his life – may that cursed Leonardo Márquez pay for his crimes!

Now Márquez rallied to Veracruz with his old comrade, General Miguel Miramón, at the head of twenty-five hundred traitors who gave their loyalty to the French! How could he find enough leaders strong of heart and willing to fight for their country, enabled by education and skill, who did not yearn to rule, themselves?

Not an easy task – yet he must.

Now he had to choose whether or not to reinstate the former presidente, Ignacio Comonfort, a man who had attempted a golpe de estado – coup –, and who had personally ordered Juárez arrested. Of course, it was not the first time he had been imprisoned for his political convictions and he had soon been released to replace the exiled Comonfort, who had sought refuge in the United States of America. Yet now Comonfort claimed a patriotic desire to defend his homeland against the intruder. Perhaps. What did he hope to gain? Best to keep him in México City with the reserves under Juárez's watchful eye.

The Presidente leaned back in his chair and stared at the map of México on the wall. So few leaders, so few resources. He would have to prove himself again through one of his greatest attributes – resilience.

WATCHING FATHER LEAVE

June 1862

"I didn't know there would be so many people" Garcia said to Juan Antonio.

They were standing in the middle of the Plaza de Armas, surrounded by their fellow Potosinos. The summer heat weighed heavily upon the crowd, and the men had been obliged to remove their sombreros so they would not obscure the view of those behind them. Because it was midday and there was a classic cloudless summer sky in the mountains, there was almost no shade and some of the onlookers had gathered on the store porches to avoid the sun.

They had assembled to watch the departure parade of the Potosíno regiment. It was the second group to be formed in the city and was comprised of mostly older men. They were to be held in reserve in the Federal District under the command of the former presidente, General Ignacio Comonfort. The forces would only see action if the French broke through the main line of defense at Puebla or bypassed the direct route to the capital. Juan Antonio's father was amongst them.

Looking out at the group, Juan Antonio felt someone staring at him. Scanning the opposite side of the square his eyes fell upon Graciana, who smiled and waved. He waved back and started to motion with his right forefinger pointing down to the center of the square and moving it a small circle while he mouthed "Hablamos después."

She smiled and nodded and hoped she understood.

"You want to talk to her afterwards?" Garcia asked.

"Sure. Why not? We haven't seen her in a while."

"De acuerdo. Makes no difference to me." Garcia replied, turning back to peer through the crowd.

After several more moments of waiting they heard the bugle of the approaching soldiers. As the men entered the plaza from the east side Juan Antonio could see many of his father's friends, but not yet his father, in their ranks. The men were marching in columns of four with a uniformed officer and standard-bearer at their head. The only armed man was the officer, whom he didn't recognize and who looked younger than the rest of the men, maybe in his thirties. The flag bearer was Señor Gutierrez, a cattle rancher. He carried the Potosíno standard against his shoulder as if it were a rifle. Both men wore blue uniforms with gold buttons down the front.

The officer's uniform was adorned with golden shoulder braids and wide golden cuffs as well as golden embroidery on the neck collar. All the soldiers wore tall black leather boots and matching white belts with a hanging white holster for a saber scabbard on the left side. Only the officer actually carried a sword.

The remainder of the soldiers were dressed in their normal clothes; some wore hats, some didn't. They marched unarmed; Juan Antonio's father had told him they would be issued arms and uniforms when they arrived at the capital. As the column drew closer the officer unsheathed his sword and marched with it against his shoulder.

The soldiers passed by in formation with their heads turned to face the crowd on the periphery of the square. When they had reached the center, they stopped and pivoted to face the Palacio del Gobierno.

The officer stamped his foot curtly then raised his sword in a salute to the flag while the flag bearer lowered his flag to point directly in front of him. The officer moved the sword across his face then raised it again. With a cry, he rested the sword against his shoulder again, the flag bearer returned the flag back to his shoulder, and the men began to file out of the plaza on the opposite side.

It was at this moment that Juan Antonio caught a glimpse of his father, Francisco Ayala, who had always done the right thing for his country and for his family, marched in front of Juan Antonio, ready to do battle. Juan Antonio deeply admired his father for this. He stared at the backs of the soldiers as to the cheers of the crowd they headed out of town.

After the soldiers had left and the townspeople were starting to disperse, Juan Antonio asked for Garcia to accompany him while he spoke with Graciana. They found her after working their way through the crowd a bit.

Graciana was a pretty young woman of seventeen. Her face had just a touch of Aztec influence – the way her nose rounded off and in the shape of her lips, rounder than the criollos whose thinner lips spoke of European influence. She was wearing a cross on a thin golden chain, and to Juan Antonio this made her look especially pretty. Although she was smiling, she seemed a little distracted and was holding the hem of her blouse in her hands.

"Hola! Did you enjoy it?" she asked Juan Antonio.

"It was fun." he replied.

Garcia greeted her with a wave. "Hi Graciana," he said.

"Your father leaves tomorrow right?" Graciana's gaze toward Juan Antonio seemed to contain sympathy.

"Yes, they camp on the outskirts of town tonight, then march south after their morning coffee."

"Will you miss him?"

"Claro! But I think he should be fine. They're sending him to the capital with the reserve units. He'll be under General Comonfort. Can you believe they let him back in? After the golpe de estado and everything else?"

"We may have guts but we have no generals." Garcia said.

"I hope they keep a close watch on him so he doesn't try anything." Graciana said. "You never know what that scoundrel could do with an army at his command."

"What are you doing tonight?" she asked, changing the subject.

"I have to work and tonight Garcia is busy. Sorry!"

Graciana expressed regret and with that they exchanged goodbyes and started to walk out of the plaza.

As they walked home Garcia said to Juan Antonio "Hey, you have to work, but I'm not doing anything tonight. Why did you say that?"

"Because." Juan Antonio responded crisply.

The abruptness of his reply left Garcia speechless.

As they left they were struck by the realization that San Luis Potosí was slowly emptying of men. Soon there would be none left, but they preferred that to being a French colony.

September 1862

It was autumn and Emperor Napoléon III was trotting his horse through the forest of Compiègne. Although he was riding, he had opted against his riding outfit and was still in the same clothing that he had worn on the carriage ride to Senlis, minus the black top hat. Despite the wind, his handlebar mustache stayed rigid and his goatee straight. Perfection in personal grooming was an individual right. He felt he really ought to compliment his barber but that would only make the man get cozy. There had not been time to change into the appropriate attire, because he felt like clearing his head of the events of the last week: the *Series* festivities with over one hundred important nobles and Parisian celebrities to be catered to; the hunts with the royals and the departure of his troops for Mexico.

His horse reached the top of the hill from where Louis-Napoléon could observe the Château of Compiègne. From the rear only the two stories could be seen but it was in essence his rural paradise. One thousand feet wide, with alternating embellished rounded or triangular pediments over the windows and drape and sash patterns carved into the stone, with niches filled with statues, it extended outward from the rear portico to the lawn edges. He reined his horse so that he could appreciate the scene in the setting sun. The temperature was falling and he could see the horse's exhalations. He owed the improvements of the château to his uncle, the grand empire builder. This was one of the finest of the properties he had inherited from his uncle. It had remained unscathed during the days of Louis XVIII, Charles X, Louis-Philippe and the days of the Second Republic.

Those idiots had all faltered because of their lack of anything imperial. They had never undertaken anything grand or worthy of a nation such as France. They rested on their haunches, copying past styles. He, Napoléon III, was the first to raise France again like the phoenix from the ashes to its glorious destiny! The imperial style was again à la mode, and France's army was unrivaled and its navy grew; soon it would challenge the British and their domination of the world's commerce.

Mobility on a worldwide scale – that was the secret. The English ruled through the illusion of invulnerability; they controlled the oceans and could move small forces anywhere and at anytime. How else could they dominate such a country as India, which had mutinied not five years ago? Soon France would have a similar navy to take the oceans and the colonies to serve her! In France railroads had been built to connect Paris to all points of the country and in the capital itself the already broad avenues were being widened for ease of movement and communication. Throughout the countryside the network of rural banks he had commissioned drew in the funds to fuel France's expansion. Never before had capital flows been so solvent.

Was this not progress? Was this not imperial?

The setting sun had covered most of the château's first story's bricks in shade, but Louis-Napoléon remained outside to absorb magnificent scene. The view of the green space of the park, with the alley of trees changing colors, terminating at the building was so symmetrically perfect it was exquisite. An imperial residence worthy of his presence!

He knew the Empress Eugénie would be reposing. She was exhausted after the strain of entertaining the five groups of invités in the past weeks. After the men's hunt and the women's card games she had been an excellent hostess at the evening balls. If only she would pay more attention to what she said and in whose company it was spoken! The faux pas she committed would be the end of her with the Paris elite. With a sigh he told himself that was what he got for marrying a Spaniard.

Now, le Mexique…

That fool Lorencez's head would roll, as well as that Mexican buffoon Almonte. Neither one knew what he was doing. Their incompetence had put the entire plan behind schedule. And even that gullible Austrian imbecile, Archduke Ferdinand Maximilian, worried they might not succeed! Everything depended upon on the capture of the capital, Mexico City. After that they would install Maximilian as Catholic emperor, leave him in charge and move on. With a little luck, the Confederate States of America might last long enough to receive support from Mexique and they would win the American civil war. Divide and conquer! He reveled in his own power.

And there was the matter of that new Prussian prime minister, or soon-to-be prime minister as his spies in the Prussian court informed him. They said he harbored territorial ambitions. He might have to be dealt with. Well, the Austrians would soon fix this danger on their flank, this Otto von Bismarck. He knew the man from the previous decade when he was Prussia's ambassador in Paris. At the time he had parlayed for a détente between the two nations.

Le Mexique…

With over thirty thousand troops there and plenty of artillery the soldiers would make short work of those Mexican upstarts. *Mexican patriotism, my eye!* he thought. France was a nation when they were still cutting the hearts out of sacrificial victims and beheading athletes! What was that ballgame the Aztecs played?

Now they thought themselves equals to France! This impudence would not go unpunished. They would see an extraction of wealth so brutal it would make them pray for the return of the Spanish encomienda system!

With a start and a flash of anger he spurred his horse toward the right side of the château and the stables. The light was fading quickly and he was hungry. Imagine that, hungry after days of eating buffets à la Russe!

THE MAN AND THE BOY

October 1862

Sunlight filled the Palacio del Gobierno in Puebla. General Jesús González Ortega stood looking out the window contemplating his assignment to defend the country against the French gabachos!

General Zaragoza – *may he rest in peace* – had fallen victim to yellow fever hardly one month ago and Juárez had appointed him as his replacement. He would never have hoped for events to transpire the way they did but he could have dreamed of this happening to him, he who had always been passed over for lack of military background. He adjusted the green sash with gold bangles that suspended his sword around his waist and unbuttoned the gold buttons on his blue jacket to loosen the flared red collar. It would not be easy to follow in Zaragoza's footsteps; there was even talk of naming Puebla after him!

Additionally the French had landed thirty thousand more men on September 22nd and the Conservatives had contributed some thousands more. They could not know the exact quantity until they marched, because these last had straggled in and were not quartered centrally.

It appeared he would have the winter to prepare and train his men, but first he needed caps for the officers and rifles for them. Presidente Juárez said the Congresso Nacional would soon issue another call for volunteers to prevent México from becoming a European colony once more. But, personally, he had determined the time had come to summon two gallant youths to his aid. He felt it prudent to invite Juan Antonio's best friend because the two could look after one another. As volunteers, he would find posts for them under his tutelage and uphold the vow he had made to Francisco Ayala to protect his only son.

Seating himself at his black wooden desk, he dipped his pen and began to write the authorization letter.

THE MARCH SOUTH

October 1862

The sun had not yet cleared the mountains when Juan Antonio and Garcia commenced their journey southward. Their trip to the capital would take ten to twelve days since there were many long gradual inclines and declines along the way on the road south. The mountains still cast shadows, and even the brush and cactuses did to a certain extent. The danger of banditos would be ever present, but the boys had decided to diverge from the highway at times and follow lesser trails when plausible.

Juan Antonio broke the silence. "It's nice to be on the road" he said.

Garcia nodded his assent.

Since receiving Ortega's letter of invitation the boys had hardly been able to contain their excitement. Of course, they were a little scared of their unknown future, but if they were to die, then what more worthy way than valiantly fighting the gabachos?

Behind them the single-story houses of the unnamed pueblo they were passing through showed increasing signs of activity; even in the cold October mountain air chickens still needed to be fed and tortillas baked. Juan Antonio pulled his poncho tighter in an attempt to stave off the morning chill. He hoped their shoes would hold out and they could beat the snow. They would be clear of the highest elevations by the fourth or fifth day. After that the slopes would head downhill. Aside from Querétaro, there were no major cities on the road, but, especially south of Querétaro, there were intermittent pueblos and aldeas – villages. One never knew, maybe a passing stagecoach would take pity on them! The cold would keep them from being too exhausted but their nights could be very difficult if they could not arrange for shelter. If not, they would find chaparral tinder for a campfire.

Despite the hardship, the boys' spirits were high as they walked. This was their first time to be truly independent, masters of their own destiny. And they shared it together! Already they felt themselves to be more like men in charge of their own futures and they were armed. Garcia had a revolver but since Francisco Ayala had taken the rifle with him, Juan Antonio had only a knife, primarily for wolves at night and possibly for banditos.

There had been a resurgence of banditos on the roads, but this was more often in the south and west of Puebla, where there were no soldiers and the terrain offered more hiding places and villagers to steal from. When they were finished with the French there would be numerous punitive expeditions to exterminate the banditos once and for all!

Where the youths walked now was brown but broken by occasional sparse vegetation. Even though the land surrounding them was not flat, they had the impression of walking on an endless highland llano that ended ahead at the crest of the next ridge, running into the striking azure sky.

In the afternoon they reached their first pueblo. They knew they were approaching a small village when they saw a stick fence and a small wooden house beside it. Outside the fence, chickens pecked at the ground aimlessly and seemed oblivious to their surroundings.

The town did not even have a proper square and the roads were quite narrow – barely a coach's width wide. Even the tiny church did not possess a bell tower. But the people the boys met were friendly and informed them of another pueblo several hours up the road that they could reach before sundown.

The next pueblo was even smaller; it was off the road and over a ridge. There were perhaps only sixteen or seventeen houses centered around a modest church which was in reality merely a plain building, undistinguished from the others except for the glass windows on the sides. After identifying themselves as traveling volunteers, they were allowed to sleep in the small horse barn of one of the residents.

When they awoke, rigid from sleeping on the earth and hay, they could still see frost on the ground. The temperature must have dropped very low during the night. At least the days were still warm. If they could just reach Querétaro before any snow fell, they would be in the clear, because as they descended from the highlands, the temperatures would quickly rise.

Almost immediately after thanking their hosts, and buying a few flour tortillas from them for breakfast and for the journey, they set off again. Their muscles were stiff, and they would need to eat a warm meal for either lunch or dinner to sustain their bodies. They had departed San Luis Potosí with only the clothes on their backs and their weapons, and had little money to pay for food along the way as well as the several nights' hotel fare in Querétaro and the capital, where they would bathe and recuperate.

That day, the scenery became more pronounced; the ridges lost their vegetation and bare rock showed. Walking at a slower pace than the previous day, the boys spoke little and there were few travelers on the road – only the occasional coach or small group of horsemen. What news they could glean was that, all along the length of this road, and many others in the country, brave men such as themselves traveled in similar circumstances – poor in possessions, rich in courage.

They were nowhere near a pueblo at midday so despite their pangs of hunger they continued until the end of the afternoon when the sun began to set and the wind grew brisker. Because they had let their sombreros hang on their backs during the day to enjoy the sun's warmth, their faces were sunburned and chapped by the wind. Fortunately, just as the light was dying, they spotted the silhouette of a town on the horizon and reached it slightly after nightfall.

They were relieved to see that the pueblo was a little larger than most and that it did have a small hotel and saloon. They would have a place to sit and rest, and the sight of townspeople in hats and jackets made them feel at ease. There was even a paved square, which served as a rest stop for the stagecoaches with the mail and passenger loads, in front of the church. The exterior paint on the buildings was pretty fresh although mostly monotone brown and orange and not as colorful as the houses in San Luis Potosí.

The saloon was very small; there were only four circular tables and no bar. The bartender just poured right at your table or in the kitchen. Juan Antonio and Garcia ordered chicken rice soup and coffee, and the warmth of the food reinvigorated them after their two days of walking.

The hotel owner was gregarious and outgoing and they explained to him where they were headed and what they were going to do. He was especially impressed by their personal letter from General Ortega. He let them have some bread for free and even arranged for them to sleep in the stables.

That night passed much better than the first because the stable was soundly built and not much chill or wind entered. In the morning the hotel owner fed them tortillas with eggs, potatoes and chili sauce, and gave them milk to drink. All this nourishment really helped their spirits. Now their stomachs would have something to burn against the cold! They were only three more days from Querétaro, according to the townspeople, and so far everything was going fine.

The third day of their trip passed very quickly because their spirits had been buoyed by the respect and hospitality shown to them in the town. They began to discuss how it felt to have a purpose, a goal, a sense of self actualization. Surely if everyone in México united and fought together, the French didn't stand a chance, no matter how many cannons or horses they had.

Around noon they found a stream close to the road and they followed it away from view until they could take a bath in private. There were a few cattle near the stream where they washed, so they knew there had to be a hacienda close by. There was sparse wind that day and they only felt cold when they crested ridges and caught the breeze directly.

By sundown that day they still had not seen a town since the one they passed in the distance shortly after their bath, and it was much too late to turn around, so they decided to build a fire. They had very little to eat, only some tortillas and some rolls from their families. This dampened their mood considerably, but they expected to be forced to sleep outdoors on the road and this would just be one of those hardships. At least they had not had snow, and if it just held off for a couple more days, they would have beaten it.

It was a simple matter for Juan Antonio and Garcia to gather brushwood and ignite a fire, and they decided to join their ponchos together and sleep next to each other to stay warm. They reckoned the best manner of survival would be for one to keep watch against wild animals while the other slept, and if the wind didn't change overnight and blow from a direction that they were not sheltered from, they would get an acceptable night's sleep.

In the end, what little wind there was did not disturb them and they were bedazzled by the stars that shone in the sky above them. It was a brisk autumn night, almost November by now, and they could see the whole marvelous expanse above them. Back home they had often gazed at the stars but always the mountain ranges had partially obscured their view. Here, free of all external influences, and together as best friends, they were quite content. The hardships they endured only deepened their feelings of camaraderie.

It was during that cold fall night in the Sierra Madres that the two young men vowed that they would never be separated on the field and that the death of one was as final as the death of them both. They would live as one and die as one.

IDEALISTS FOLLOWING THEIR HEARTS

October 1862

Juan Antonio and Garcia slept very lightly that night and stirred well before sunrise. They were almost out of food and would need another hot meal at the first aldea they found. Fortunately they had not spent very much money since San Luis Potosí, so they would be able to afford hotels in Querétaro and México City.

As soon as the sun was high enough in the sky, they arranged their possessions, tried to limber up their stiffened muscles, and continued on their way. The wind was rising and the temperature had fallen significantly. The clouds were low and grey; snow might fall. Garcia had started to sneeze and both adolescents felt weakened although they were not discouraged.

Luck was with them on this day and they reached a pueblo by midmorning.

They walked straight to the plaza and found a hotel that did serve food. It was an interesting hotel, built with a wooden façade in the norteamericano style, yet inside hung a large, ornate chandelier imported from France. There was also a tall standing pendulum clock and coffee grinders imported from the United States. The boys decided to have an early lunch because their strength was low and their funds were comfortable. They ate a meal of coffee, hard rolls, beans and bacon. It was expensive, but the sensation of overly hot bacon going down their throats was delectable and the fat in it would burn hot in their systems and warm them against the elements.

According to the innkeeper there were now two more villages on the road and they were less than fifty miles from Querétaro. They would not have to concern themselves with sleeping outdoors because from here on out the population in the center of the country was denser.

After the early lunch, the pair left again and followed the road to Querétaro. True to what they had been told, there were many villages now and the traffic was heavier. Although they were still in the highlands, the route passed between the mountains now and the going was smoother.

They spent the evening in a pueblo where a family let them use the hut of a field hand who had left to fight at Puebla for the cinco de Mayo victory. Juan Antonio let Garcia have the simple bed and he slept on the floor. It was Garcia's first bed in four nights! The next morning they washed with some heated water from a kettle and continued their journey.

For the last day of the first leg of their journey the way was mostly downhill and they made good time. Around eleven in the morning they spotted Querétaro from a hilltop, and after walking several more hours, they began to pass huts with wooden fences for livestock on either side of the road.

Querétaro was a fairly large city and would have all the necessary amenities; hotels, food, and a stagecoach station where they might even be able to afford a ticket to México City. The streets were relatively crowded when they entered the city, and they headed for the main plaza so they could get a hotel room there to soak in a hot bath, shave and rest for the night.

The sun was still high in the sky and they could see the beauty of the city. The streets were broader than in San Luis Potosí and the house exteriors favored lighter pastels, or even white as opposed to the reds and other lush colors of the Potosíno region. The Cathedral was a beautiful structure with ornamental buttresses tied into the building, and with many fountains next to it. On the roof was an ornamental parapet, punctuated by pyramidal posts. The residents kept their streets meticulously clean and a fair number of the houses were two-story buildings. They had definitely left the mountain towns behind.

Walking past the Cathedral they saw a soldier in full regalia with a holstered revolver hanging from his white belt. He was just removing his field cap to wipe the sweat from his brow and did not seem overly concerned with appearances, so the boys judged him to be very approachable. They inquired as how best to get to Puebla and if there were any convoys heading south with which they might hitch a ride. The soldier replied that if they went to the coach station early in the morning and declared themselves volunteers who were traveling to enlist, the coach driver would offer them empty seats for half fare to the capital. Once in México City, if they couldn't find troops to march with, then they could probably try the same thing again there. There was only one coach a day so it was advisable to get there as early as possible because at most only one or two seats a day were open, including the driver's bench.

This seemed the most logical course of action and they resolved to do this first thing the following day. After making that decision, they headed to a hotel that the soldier had recommended. It was a smaller and more spartan establishment than the one in the square, and the rooms were windowless and barely accommodated two single beds. On the wooden table in the room was a pitcher for washing their hands and face.

Exhausted from the journey, the pair went straight to bed.

THE STAGECOACH

November 1862

The following morning the young men left before sunrise, missing coffee, and made their way to the stagecoach station. The temperature had dropped and there was a brisk wind. Even so, it still was not as cold in the city as in the mountains.

They were the first to arrive after the stable boy, who was already rigging the horses to the coach. He was a nice boy who told them their chances would be pretty good because most of the volunteers had already come through and it was a sizable coach.

It was indeed large. The harness could hold six horses, although the boy was only hitching four to it. There were benches at both the front and the rear of the stagecoach, which were where they would have to sit if they got on at all. Those seats were never in high demand in the winter months because the exposure to the weather could make it a chilly experience.

The coach was brown and had a very utilitarian look to it. The wheels were identical size and the exterior benches were mounted very high. The thoroughbraces hung very low, about as close to the ground as the boys had ever seen. Inside eight people could sit comfortably – twelve if they all squeezed in – because the center bench that could accommodate up to six and each outer bench three. Luggage was carried on the top.

The stable boy liked talking to them. He was younger than they were – sixteen to be exact. He feared the French might break through Puebla and then besiege the capital. If the capital fell then the French armies would certainly march north and west, and they would take Querétaro.

Juan Antonio and Garcia assured him that General Ortega would never let this happen, and he in turn swore to die as a guerrilla, fighting against the French in the hills. Apparently, many people in Querétaro had already pledged to flee the city and fight from the hills should the city fall.

After they had spoken to the boy for some time, the stationmaster arrived. He told them they would have to wait and see if the coach filled, and if it didn't, they could ride outside for half fare because they were enlisting.

Nine passengers showed up and the interior filled, but it did not overfill, and just before they were set to leave, the driver said they could purchase their tickets and climb on the rear bench. Saying Adios to the stable boy, they climbed up the wheel and onto the rear bench, settling in for the easy ride to México City. There would be only two overnight stops on this trip, and passengers who couldn't afford the price of a hotel room at the stops usually spent the night with the horses in the stables.

Relieved from the strain of walking and by their good fortune in securing a ride to the capital, Juan Antonio and Garcia began to talk freely as they headed south. Since the stagecoach was larger, it jostled less than one would expect. The terrain was not as dramatic as what they had seen so far, and the soil color lightened a little. There was also more vegetation and trees than in the higher altitudes.

The first day of the journey was uneventful; the coach stopped several times a day to switch horses and to allow the passengers to stretch their legs. They were a mixed bunch. There was a family of four returning home to the capital, three single men traveling independently and a couple. Juan Antonio and Garcia were able to speak with the other passengers only briefly at these stops and before the others checked into their rooms at night; the boys slept in the stables. But, by the second day all the passengers were familiar with one another, and on their second night the boys even paid for a small cramped second-story hotel room because they had almost reached the capital and had more money than they needed for room and board there.

It was on the third day, when the trail started to wind its way through the mountains encircling the capital, that the coach rapidly crested a hill and the boys heard the passengers start to talk excitedly. Looking over the front of the carriage Juan Antonio and Garcia found themselves staring down at México City. They had almost finished their journey!

When they arrived at the stagecoach station the boys climbed down from the rear bench, thanked the driver, and bade the other passengers farewell.

"Well, we're here ahead of schedule" Juan Antonio said to Garcia. "Let's go check in with my mother's friend Señora Muñoz and see if we can locate my father." He was anxious to see his father.

As they wandered through the city, they noticed the mood there was much more hurried and tense than it had been during their previous visit. Back then, the war had seemed near certain yet the true understanding of its consequences had not fully sunken in. Now, in spite of their tremendous victory at Puebla, the citizens of México City knew that this was only the beginning and that a bitter fight lay ahead of them. The city was also animated by the presence of troops, but since they were mostly older men, they were very orderly and courteous.

Señora Muñoz knew about General Ortega's letter and was expecting them, albeit not for several more days. When they arrived, she was delighted to see them and set about arranging their bedding and preparing a hot meal of beans and beef in a tortilla. When they inquired as to the whereabouts of Juan Antonio's father, she told them where he was barracked and that he was even allowed to visit her occasionally. Even though it was the end of the afternoon they resolved to go talk to him.

When they got to the barracks, they had to identify themselves to the sentries in the street and give Francisco Ayala's name to a soldier, who said he would try to find him. These soldiers had rifles and uniforms, which was an encouraging sign for the two, although the tall hats they wore were from the war with the United States fifteen years ago. Hopefully their rifles were more modern.

They spotted Juan Antonio's father Francisco walking through the interior of the building and when he emerged father and son embraced.

"Ay, mi hijo. How are you?"

"I'm great, Papa. I'm great. We didn't have any problems getting here, it all went pretty well."

"Not too cold?"

"Oh no, not really."

"And you Garcia, you're looking well. How is everything?"

"I'm good. The trip was pretty easy. Like Juan Antonio said, we didn't hit any problems."

"Mira, I'm supposed to be here in the barracks but let me see if I can get somebody to cover for me. You'll have to wait here. Don't run away! God, it's great to see you!"

The boys said they would not wander off and Juan Antonio's father returned to the barracks. About five minutes later he re-emerged.

"It's not going to be possible tonight, boys. Maybe tomorrow during the day. There's really no place they could tell the Captain

I was that would be credible. But, we can still talk here, next to the door." He shrugged as he finished his last sentence.

"That's okay. All we need to do is to see you anyway. And we can pass by tomorrow" Juan Antonio said, glancing sideways at Garcia, who nodded emphatically and added, "Yes, no problem. So how are things in the army?"

"Oh, we're just waiting around here. They say I could get a uniform in a few months but at least I have some new boots for drilling. General Comonfort always has us practicing marching and charging, marching and firing in formation and then more marching. But, hey, I've lost weight, right?"

"Yes, Padre, I can tell. I guess it's a good thing they have you marching nonstop."

"Well, if the French break through at Puebla, we'll probably march on the road to meet them. No one wants to fight in the capital and we're not protected by forts here like Puebla. Even if they do break through at Puebla it should cost them so dearly that even a bunch of viejos like us will send them back to Paris!" The three men laughed.

"Do all the men have rifles?" Garcia asked.

"Hardly. And the artillery we do have dates from Waterloo. Ironic, isn't it? The British sold us cannons taken from Napoléon Bonaparte in 1815 and we end up using them against his nephew fifty years later! What goes around comes around I guess. They're not as long-range but the gabachos have already learned what happens to them when they come up close."

They stepped back to let two soldiers exit the barracks. The pair of men waved to Juan Antonio's father saying "Que pasa, Francisco?"

Juan Antonio's father continued. "Anyway, as I was saying. We don't outnumber the French anymore, not after the new army that landed at Veracruz six weeks ago. They might break through Puebla. I know if there's one man who can stop them it's General Ortega. You got his letter, right?"

"Claro! I always carry it with me. That way no one ever questions our intentions or doubts that we're enlisting."

"Good. Now, here's how you'll get to Puebla. Every day there are supply trains that leave here. They move very slowly so it always takes them four days to get there with the loaded wagons. You could actually get there faster on foot, but you would tire yourselves out. They expect a siege, so they're sending as many provisions as possible to the city. Get to the quartermaster's depot by the Ciudela, south of town; you know where it is right?"

Both boys nodded.

"Get there about five o'clock in the morning, show your letter to the highest ranking officer you can find, and hitch a ride with them. It'll be slow but free and they'll feed you. They might even issue you equipment. The sooner you arrive at Puebla, the better your odds of being issued a rifle. Of course, you can always take one off a gabacho!"

"Sounds good, Padre. We'll try tomorrow. We don't want to inconvenience Señora Muñoz."

"Yes. You express my gratitude to her for letting you boys stay and for the meals she cooks for me. And give my very best to Ortega when you get there! You will have to tell him to treat you two well for me! He will be your surrogate father in my absence."

Juan Antonio's father smiled reservedly as he said this. Juan Antonio abruptly realized how being a soldier had changed his father; his manner had become more direct and brusque. And he, Juan Antonio, was being pushed into manhood.

"We will, Padre. We will."

THE DEPOT

November 1862

The following morning Juan Antonio and Garcia woke up very early and departed the home of Señora Muñoz after snacking on bread and milk. They made their way through the quiet streets to the supply depot on the south side of the city. The streets were empty, and it was spooky as neither of the young men had ever been in a city so large at a time when it was totally silent.

But as they drew nearer to the army depot, they began to hear the sounds of activity, and soon they saw, framed by the rising sun on the outskirts of the city, dozens of tents with men moving purposefully about them. Some were leading horses to wagons while others lugged sacks of flour and coffee. There were at least ten wagons and it appeared they would be leaving soon. Walking into the hustle of activity, the boys spotted an officer standing by the wagons supervising the loading.

Approaching him, Juan Antonio said "Buenos días, Señor. We are headed to Puebla to volunteer. We have a personal invitation letter from General Ortega himself."

A look of surprise crossed the officer's face when Juan Antonio mentioned the letter, and the man stared at them for a moment.

"Bueno. Help these men stow the provisions and march with them. When the burros need to be unhitched and watered, you help the men. They'll feed you dinner and you can draw bedding."

"Yes sir" Juan Antonio said. "And what can you tell us of the French?"

"The French? We're in a hurry. They're already on the move as of over a week ago. Not their main force but two columns coming up the Jalapa and Cordoba roads. We already fought them at the mesa of Cerro Gordo where we tried to halt the norteamericanos in forty-seven. We think they might attack before Christmas. So, you men will have your plates full. Now, help out loading." With that the officer turned and walked over to the adjacent wagon.

The boys started assisting, hoisting the sacks onto the wagons, and when the convoy was ready they walked slowly along with it.

Destination: Puebla!

MIRAMAR

November 1862

Close to Trieste, in the Austro-Hungarian Empire, on the balcony of a beautiful castle called Miramar, Archduke Ferdinand Maximilian, younger brother to the Emperor Francis Joseph of Austria-Hungary, stared at the waves of the Adriatic Sea lapping the shore. He was lost in thought.

Delays, delays, delays! He should be in Mexico City by now! The French had overestimated the amount of enthusiasm for a Catholic emperor in Mexico. They had told him flowers would be tossed before their soldiers and that the Mexicans were begging for intervention. They certainly hadn't thrown flowers at Puebla!

Before he could assume the throne there, he would need to be positive of full compliance by the population as well as the complete underwriting of the endeavor by the French and his older brother. He would demand a plebiscite, and without the unequivocal support of his future subjects he would not go.

A cold wind came off the water and blew against his face. He shivered involuntarily and turned to walk indoors. One of his servants was in the library and he bade him good morning in German.

"Guten morgen, Your Excellency. How are you feeling today?"

"In good health, danke." Maximilian replied. As he turned away from the servant he caught a glimpse of his profile in the mirror. At thirty one, he already had a receding hairline, partially compensated for by a dramatic part to the left side. Consequently, he always maintained his handlebar mustache and chest-length beard in pristine condition. At six feet, two inches, he cut an imposing figure, yet his blue eye revealed the naiveté and absent-mindedness in his nature. He had recently overheard a duchess gossiping about how he seemed to have a stupid brooding stare. Let them see if they would call him stupid when he sat on the Mexican throne! He always had been denied what should be his also, the Austro-Hungarian throne. Cursed primogeniture!

Retired as commander-in-chief of the navy and as governor-general of Lombardo-Venetia, he sat in his idyllic palace of Miramar and twiddled his thumbs while his brother commanded one of the mightiest powers in the world! Meanwhile the courts tittered and whispered of his incompetence.

Why, had they not yanked him from power in northern Italy prior to the French campaign; their successive defeats at the hands of Napoléon III and Vittorio Emmanuele, at the time leader of the Sardinians, events would have transpired differently. It was his own people's brutality perpetrated against the Italians for five generations that culminated in the explosion of rage on the fields at Solferino; in a single day thirty-two thousand men massacred one another, even bayoneting the wounded as they lay on the field bleeding. His prior measures meant to reconcile the gulf between the Italians and the Austrians had been meeting with mounting success prior to the war.

His steps quickened and he was inadvertently gesturing with his hands as he walked down the corridor. Just then he passed by the bedchamber of the young Archduchess Marie Charlotte Amélie, daughter of the king of Belgium. Since his retirement, they did not share the same bedroom. It must be difficult for her in the European courts; Belgium was barely thirty years old, and here she was, embarrassed by her husband. Well, his time in the sun was fast approaching. They would not dismiss him so lightly!

PUEBLA

November 1862

The boys' ride in the convoy passed uneventfully as they accompanied the wagon train to Puebla, integrating themselves into the rest of the troop of soldiers. Additionally, the two found men from San Luis Potosí that said there was a rifle battalion that had already been sent as the first wave.

The rush of volunteers had mostly slowed down by then; it was only due to their young age and the deliberate stalling by General Ortega that they were coming in behind the rest.

Upon their arrival Ortega had seen to it that they had beds to sleep in and were assigned as pages to his field staff. This did not mean they were non-combatants, but it assured Ortega that they would be well taken care of and not exposed to harm unnecessarily. The boys informed him of their oath and he promised to never separate them.

Puebla was a medium-sized city with architecture quite similar to the capital: rows of arched windows over balconies and thick stone walls. Most buildings had three or four stories. The central plaza was very large and could be used to organize troop formations and artillery transports. Most importantly, Puebla was protected by a circle of nine forts, all of which were manned. On the cinco de Mayo the French had charged from the east from the roads, attacking the forts of Loreto and Guadalupe on Guadalupe Hill. These forts were the most heavily garrisoned and fortified.

Daily the soldiers worked to prepare the forts and supplies were delivered from the capital regularly. The size of the army, however, was such they were only able to stockpile supplies at a slow rate. This was worsened by the fact that General Ortega was often forced to pay the men in supplemental food due to lack of funds and the government could not afford such an expense at one time, be it paid monetarily or in provisions.

If the forts fell, the soldiers had sworn to defend Puebla, street by street, house by house. Everyone knew if Puebla fell, México would fall. The French were sending five times as many troops this time – they were not likely to charge blindly uphill against the fronts of the forts again – and General Comonfort's reserves, outgunned and outnumbered as they were, could not hope to contain the French in the open field.

The forts were in part under the command of a visiting Italian general named Ghilardi, who went from fort to fort dictating orders in Italian. Usually one could understand him, but if not, Colonel Columbres of the Ingenhieros would tell them what to do. Ghilardi had earned his credentials fighting for the short-lived Republic of Rome in 1848 and 1849; he'd helped defend the city against a similar type of siege.

For the most part, the boys did not have to dig deep trenches or erect palisades. In general, they acted as couriers between General Ortega, in the city center, and the outlying forts, allowing them to see the famous forts of Guadalupe and Loreto.

Guadalupe was smaller than Loreto but could reasonably contain several hundred soldiers. Circular turrets for cannon platforms were at all four corners of the fort and in the flat stretches five-foot thick stone walls there were firing gaps for the cannons. The fort was surrounded by a deep trench.

Loreto was substantially stronger than Guadalupe. In addition to the cannon platforms at each corner, there were narrow firing squares spaced evenly in every wall, through which soldiers could maneuver their rifles. They could stay standing on a platform inside the walls of the fort and shoot without exposing their bodies to hostile fire. And the walls were the height of perhaps four men, making scaling much harder.

The weeks passed in this manner; the men reinforcing the forts and training, the boys delivering messages, and the generals strategizing. Christmas passed, then the New Year, and no attack came.

The Mexcian forces learned that the main body of the French army had advanced beyond the town of Perote and that they had been struck by guerrillas from Puebla. Closer to the city, where the two roads to the Gulf Coast met, the French had reunited and stopped, waiting for the spring.

Up north, the norteamericanos were still embroiled in their War of the States, which showed no signs of ending soon.

Shortly after New Year's Day 1863, General Ortega posted the January 1 issue of *El Siglo XIX,* which had just arrived. In it, the journalists dedicated an article to the defenders of the nation stating:

"The Independence and dignity of the Republic, the continued struggle against foreign invasion until we emerge victorious, the upholding of the Constitution of 1857 and the Reform Laws, the consolidation of law and order, the perfection of the representative system with the express aim of the enforcement of liberty, the representative system and the well being of our people, such do we pledge for the people."

The soldiers who read this understood that, if the French broke them here, all that they had achieved through decades of struggle would be lost again to European subjugation. Their will was resolute and many swore to see victory or die trying. And so the men waited...

February 1863

"Mind your step, Your Highness." the footman said to Emperor Napoléon III.

Napoléon removed his top hat and stepped carefully onto the lowered carriage step then into the carriage interior where the Empress Eugénie was settling in.

The carriage was a magnificent vehicle; huge black wheels with gold ornamented hubs, a silver-plated retractable foot step, glass windows with plush satin curtains and tufted cushions for the occupants. The exterior of the carriage had gold embellishment and crests all over the top and the side edges and the wood was painted the shiniest black. The outriders were painted green and gold in honor of the Empress.

The Emperor placed his walking stick on the carriage floor and threw his coat off with a shrug of his shoulders. His servant caught it, and laid it on the cushion beside the Emperor. When they heard the footmen securing their latest purchases on the roof of the carriage that followed behind theirs the Emperor said "Excellent store isn't it? You know Monsieur Boucicault told me the Bon Marché sold almost seven million francs worth of merchandise in 1862?"

The Empress responded in her accented French. "Oh yes, I adore shopping here. They have everything."

The Emperor did not usually accompany his wife for such shopping excursions; he typically left the selection of table clocks and petticoats up to her. But, he could not wait to try out their latest purchase – flushing toilets, imported straight from England! A recent invention by a Mr. Thomas Crapper, Englishman. Now Eugénie would have much more to display than just another enameled comb or a jeweled snuffbox!

Their coach sagged slightly as the pair of liverymen assigned to their carriage stepped onto the rear platform. The driver snapped the reins and the carriages began to make their way through the square past the three-, four- and five-story buildings along Rue de Babylonne.

On their way out of the seventh arrondissement they stopped by the Hôtel des Invalides to pay their respects to his uncle. The carriages pulled to a stop in Place Vauban before the dome that sheltered the ashes of his uncle, Napoléon Bonaparte. It was hardly a year ago that they had been transferred to the dome for final repose under the massive cupola. It was bitterly cold that day as it was today. Twenty horses had drawn the coffin with the ashes before a hushed multitude. It had been a time for deep reflection on France's Imperial past.

He, Napoléon III, would return France to her days of glory! The Tricolore would rule the world! This is what his people yearned for and he would grant them this boon. His prominence depended upon his ability to provide the French nation with glory and victory.

He stepped out of the coach and into the winter snow of Paris. The pale winter sun was already low in the sky and the dome cast a long shadow which eclipsed the carriages and cast a pall over their entourage. In a flash, Napoléon III, Emperor of France, realized that no matter what he accomplished in his life he would never get out from under his uncle's shadow.

EXPECT THE UNEXPECTED

March 8, 1863

On March 8th, 1863, word reached the forces at Puebla that the French columns had arrived at Amozoc again. Ortega telegraphed Congreso to let them know the battle would start very soon.

Eight days later, the soldiers on the ramparts of the fort of Guadalupe sighted the first French soldiers advancing onto the Hacienda de la Manzanilla, directly facing the Cerros de Guadalupe and de Amahucan. General Gayoso felt free to climb to the top of the wall because the French were not staging an assault but merely securing the area. With his field telescope he counted over 25,000 soldiers, including cavalry, and more than 150 cannons – a force superior to the Mexicans in quantity of troops but not in artillery. The force moved with deliberate caution and stayed well out of the cannon range of the defenders. Of course, with only 18 cannons in the fort of Guadalupe, a cannon duel would be suicide.

This move by the French had been anticipated, and, for this reason, in spite of its smaller size, the fort of Guadalupe was heavily armed. Many expected the French to take the most direct route again, this time with more caution, and the next several days confirmed this prediction, as the French were seen digging in.

Juan Antonio and Garcia attempted to secure courier assignments to this fort as often as possible to be sure they could try to participate in the defense. But contrarily, General Ortega frustrated their plans by instructing to keep them on call in the plaza as frequently as possible.

Since learning of the French force's arrival the generals held numerous staff meetings, but as everything was playing out as predicted they did not deviate from their predetermined plans and the meetings were always brief. This all changed on March 17th, when the French sent dual columns of approximately ten thousand men, each, marching northwest and southwest at a distance of two cannon shots – close enough to discern the insignia on their uniforms through a telescope, yet too distant to attack without a sortie from the fort.

Though they moved extremely slowly over the canyons surrounding the forts and towed their cannons behind wagons or carried some disassembled, by midday on March 18th the French had cut off the roads and severed the telegraph line to México City. French soldiers were positioned on all of the nearby hills; Puebla was besieged. After this the French began to entrench themselves and concentrate more to the west.

On the evening of the nineteenth a more serious generals' meeting was called. Present, were close to two dozen generals, lieutenant colonels and captains. Due to the size of the group and the need to see the map in the center of the room, the officers arranged themselves around a central table in the foyer of the Palacio del Gobierno. As dispatch couriers, Juan Antonio and Garcia had the right to be in the corridor adjoining the foyer, next to the door. Consequently, they were able to eavesdrop on the majority of the discussion.

General Ortega opened the meeting projecting his voice deeply.

"Señores. I invited all of the ranking commanders tonight because, as you know, the focal point of the French appears now to be shifting to the west. Today General Forey was seen setting up his tent on the Cerro de San Juan and their forces seem to be concentrating before the fort of Iturbide. We must address their change of strategy. General Antillon, do you have any additional observations from the west?"

"Sí. Con licenza, General. They have also transported the majority of their field pieces to San Juan. I believe it is clear that they do not intend to strike from the east but instead from the west. Puebla fell from the west in the Guerra de la Reforma. I recommend an immediate reinforcing of the forts of Iturbide and Demócrata, including the transfer of as many cannons, obuses, and mortars as can be spared from the other forts. In Iturbide we have ten field guns, in Demócrata, seventeen. Assuming they will leave some artillery dispersed throughout the rest of the ring, I predict they will bring to bear the majority of their artillery against us – say one hundred guns. Twenty-seven guns would soon be silenced by one hundred guns. I request this be taken under formal consideration."

"Your opinion is most respected, General Antillon, and we will consider reinforcement of the western forts." General Ortega replied. "However, we cannot disregard the possibility of there being two simultaneous attacks, a general attack and a diversionary one. If so, which would be the diversion? I must consider the welfare of the nine forts as a whole and as such cannot commit to the lengthy transfer of artillery between forts. Does anyone wish to comment?"

The audacious Porfirio Díaz, who with his brother Felix, was a hero from the first battle of Puebla, spoke up. "I repeat my suggestion of the previous days that we attack the gabachos in the hills at one of their weak points. They are still not fully established and we could inflict significant damage on them while they are stretched out."

"My stance on this matter has not changed," Ortega said. "We cannot be overly optimistic of our capacities against this army. This is the finest army in the world, defending on high ground with artillery that is superior to ours in rifling, accuracy and reach. Our troops could not rely on artillery support and, above all, we are fighting a defensive war. Skirmishes as such would only deplete the men and ammunition we need to outlast the French. Our objective should be to break their backs on our strongpoints, not to conduct risky offensives."

He paused slightly, squaring his shoulders and shifting his weight before continuing. "Is there anybody else?"

"What soldiers we send to Iturbide?" It was clearly General Ghilardi, speaking in an accented blend of Italian and Spanish.

General Antillon spoke again. "Sir, I too am of the opinion that a bold sortie would be successful. It is what the French would least expect of us now."

The others agreed; most appeared to favor the element of surprise.

"Frankly, we all expected it to come to this," said General Ortega, "and our secondary line of defense at the square and church strongpoints will most likely see action. We cannot avoid this with the weight of the army they have. But I repeat; we must fight defensively."

There was a moment's pause, then he continued. "Knowing a breach will most certainly occur in the primary circle, does anyone know of any weak spots that we have not considered, especially on the west side?' He was met by complete silence.

"Well, I think we have a day, perhaps two, before they hit us. But when they do, we must be prepared on every side. That is all. Thank you."

The officers started to walk out of the room, talking one to another. Juan Antonio and Garcia stood erect as the officers filed past them. As the Díaz brothers passed them they overheard part of their conversation.

"... like a turtle in a shell. We should have met them on the coastal roads and prevented them from reaching the highlands. That way they would have died of the heat." "The gabachos will pin us in..." the Díaz brothers had moved ahead and other conversations overpowered theirs now.

The youths waited for the room to clear which took about five minutes. Finally, it was empty and they reported to General Ortega.

"Any messages, General?" asked Juan Antonio.

"Yes, inform Quartermaster General Mendoza's staff that I have ordered the fort at Iturbide to receive full rations from now on, as well as supplemental ammunition, cannon shot, and sandbags. Then carry this to the Iturbide and return immediately. I don't want you two to hang around there, understood?"

"Yes, General," the two responded in unison. And with that, the two left the hall and headed for the depot to carry out their instructions.

THE FORT OF ITURBIDE

March 19, 1863

As the boys walked through the streets of Puebla, the gravity of the situation was evident all around them. None of the townspeople were in the streets and the soldiers that they passed en route to the Quartermaster General's office seemed very somber. They delivered the message and then left to deliver General Ortega's message to the fort of Iturbide. They did not know the western defenses very well because they had focused on the famous eastern forts, expecting the fighting to occur there.

As they walked Garcia asked Juan Antonio "Do you think we'll hold out? I mean twenty-four thousand men against twenty-five to thirty thousand?"

"I think so. We have the forts and the cannons, you know."

"Yes, but the cannons are so outdated."

"Still, the gabachos will have to come close to get us won't they?"

"I suppose."

Upon entering the fort, they walked in front of the Convent of San Javier which had now been converted to a strongpoint inside of Iturbide. It was a two-story hexagonal building with thick walls protecting the dome inside; it was perfectly suited for its present use and Juan Antonio wondered if the priests and nuns who had lived there had ever remotely imagined this. The fort itself was rectangular and the western side had a double bastion wall. They announced themselves to the officer on duty who was on the fringes of a campfire adjacent to the west wall. General Antillon had not yet returned to the fort so they were the first to bring the good tidings.

"At last we'll have enough to eat!" exclaimed the officer in charge.

The two youths wished to ingratiate themselves with this group so they could be present for the combat. Juan Antonio spoke first.

"Yeah, it's not the general's fault you know. He has to pay in food what they can't pay in salary and now they're running low on provisions."

"Yes, yes," the officer said gruffly. "We all know. But that doesn't fill our bellies."

Wishing to deflect his negativity, Juan Antonio asked, "Where are you from?"

"I'm from Guanajuato, as are all of us here."

"The silver-mining city, home of Manuel Doblado! Do you know him?" "Not personally. But…Viva La Reforma!"

Juan Antonio glanced around him. Many of the soldiers had white uniform pants with blue caps while others had only their own clothing; they wore sombreros and crossed ammunition belts over their chests. The officer's insignia identified him from the Second Infantry battalion of Guanajuato.

"Mira, we deliver a lot of messages and we're quick. When the shooting starts we won't be afraid, so in the future we can stay here and wait for your messages if you'd like." Garcia offered.

"Sure, if you want. You men have weapons?"

"I have my pistol but he has only a knife," Garcia replied.

"Well, it makes no difference to me. Suit yourselves."

The boys thanked him and the officer turned away.

As they left the campfire Garcia said to Juan Antonio, "All we have to do is get all the dispatches for the west and we can be here when it starts."

THE SKIRMISH

March 21, 1863

Two more days came and went and the boys befriended the soldiers, composed of the Second and Sixth infantry battalions of Guanajuato, who waited in the Iturbide fort. As the French tightened their noose around the city, concern mounted over the lack of supplies.

General Ortega had originally planned to have provisions for a siege of three months, but when they took final stock, he realized that, after having paid soldiers in food, their food had dwindled so much that they would not have enough to last them half that time. In response, two cavalry brigades were sent out to forage and collect what livestock and food remained on the surrounding homesteads.

Meanwhile, the French west of Iturbide continued digging a network of trenches. Juan Antonio and Garcia were permitted to observe this from the inner bastion, although General Antillon never loaned his field glasses to anyone and was privy to General Ortega's preference for the young men and their safety. The Mexicans could do nothing but observe the French as they dug and drew closer to the fort. It was evident they were preparing firing platforms in the trenches, and when they got to within one thousand feet, they could be heard working at night. Although they longed to fire at the French diggers, the soldiers' instructions were to fire only if fired upon as their strategy was victory through attrition.

On March 24th French cannons opened up on the fort of Iturbide.

The Mexican batteries responded and after only ten minutes the French ceased firing. At the time, Juan Antonio and Garcia were waiting in the main square for any dispatches and they heard the firing in the distance. As soon as the reports were heard, everyone stopped and then began to scurry about or head straight back to their units. For approximately half an hour the garrison believed the offensive had begun.

The boys requested dispatches to the west but all of the messages for the Iturbide were given to other couriers. They suspected Ortega had a hand in this to keep them safe. Their only mission was to deliver a communiqué to the adjacent fort of Morelos. They visited their Guanajuatan acquaintances in the Iturbide fort during the evening and stayed until ten o'clock. Everyone confirmed that, despite a brief barrage, there had been no more activity.

The following day was marked by intermittent bombardments of both the Iturbide and the Morelos forts, and when the two youths were at Iturbide in the evening the soldiers told to them the French had inched their trenches even closer to their bastions. They could hear the clanking of the digging tools in the night air as well as fragments of orders in French that the wind intermittently carried. Every one knew that the assault would come in the next few days. It was only a matter of time.

The morning of March 26th the boys and six other youths were in their shared room sleeping when they were awakened by a barrage of cannon fire. The young dispatch runners who were all in their nightclothes looked at each other then started to scramble for their clothes and dispatch bags.

Juan Antonio looked at Garcia. "This is it now. They'll charge soon. We have to get there."

The barrage continued and, judging by the noise, was very powerful. It came from the west and was certainly concentrated on the Iturbide. It took the pair maybe five minutes to get dressed and report for duty. During this time the bombardment had been an uninterrupted wall of sound in the distance.

Entering the staff headquarters Juan Antonio and Garcia found all the generals except Ortega agitatedly and scribbling notes as rapidly as they could. Reporting to the captain at the dispatch table they inquired to where they would run messages.

"Juan Antonio, you run this to Colonel Auza in Morelos right now. Collect any communications they have and come back. No hanging around to see the battle!" The captain gave him a stern look.

"Garcia, you run to Hidalgo and tell General Ghilardi his orders stand, and pick up whatever messages they have."

Grabbing the letter and placing it in his bag, Juan Antonio walked to the door.

"Juan Antonio, remember our oath!" It was Garcia, following him out.

"I'll try." said Juan Antonio, breaking into a sprint as he stepped out the door into the street. The cannon fire had not relented and was still quite loud. Juan Antonio estimated that dozens of cannons must be dueling out there.

As he ran through the nearly deserted streets, to the west he could see the trails of smoke created by the cannons to the west. It was still very early, maybe five thirty in the morning and the French would definitely storm the fort at sunrise. He wondered if they would storm Morelos also.

When he arrived at the Morelos, neighbor of the Iturbide, he saw the artillery crews on the wall, firing and reloading, firing and reloading. The men worked like machines. They would clear the breech, insert the charge, then load the cannonball and ignite the charge. They had ten cannons, some very small four- and eight-centimeter-bore bronze cannons on small wooden mounts, as well as half a dozen twelve- to twenty-four-centimeter-bore cannons in thick wooden wheeled carriages. The fort didn't have any mortars, only cannons.

The men worked frantically to fire their guns down at the trenches outside Iturbide. These crews worked without return fire from the French and although Juan Antonio could not see the Iturbide from the interior plaza, his ears told him that it was catching hell. The soldiers did not let him report to their general, but took his bag and told him to tell General Ortega that they were engaging the enemy with artillery and were not being fired upon. Iturbide, however, was being demolished.

Running back to the center of town he passed a horse-drawn wagon led by a mounted rider going to the Iturbide as fast as possible. On the wagon, cannonballs were stacked next to kegs of gunpowder. Still, the firing in the distance did not abate. The rider did not even glance at Juan Antonio as he sped by.

When Juan Antonio got to the headquarters, he found a line of sentries at duty in front of it. Inside he saw Ortega in the middle of the room, pacing. His head was bowed and his chin was propped on his left hand with his right hand supporting his left elbow. The general snapped out of his reverie and noticed Juan Antonio.

"Juan Antonio, where did they send you?"

"To Morelos, but they didn't have any messages. They just wanted me to tell you that they are firing at the enemy cannons aimed at Iturbide and not receiving return fire. Iturbide, on the other hand, is bearing the full brunt of their artillery."

"Yes, we know. They are focusing on reducing one point. We predict a charge soon. I don't know if the fort can hold. How is the ammunition supply at Morelos?"

"They seemed all right and nobody mentioned being short."

"Look, I want you to report to the reserve battalion that is forming on the west side. I need men and if you fight bravely and don't endanger yourself you'll be fine. They are to stand until nightfall and then if there is still no attack you will rejoin the runners until further orders. De acuerdo?"

"Yes, sir!" With that, Juan Antonio put down his dispatch pouch in the hallway and headed to the reserve unit, which had been brought up from the central plaza to a plaza on the western edge of the city. It was composed of several hundred men from the reserve cavalry or various other units. The men formed ranks, held fast, and awaited orders

The artillery duel continued throughout the morning, and it was quite clear the French, with their brutally effective salvos of grapeshot and heavy cannonballs, were winning. Around noon the firing died down. At first everyone was extremely tense, anticipating the cries and gunshots of an assault but there were no such sounds. After an hour or so of nervous waiting the officers allowed the men to prop their rifles in tripods and relax.

Milling about in the plaza, Juan Antonio spotted Garcia and approached to talk to him.

Garcia spoke as Juan Antonio laid down his rifle and lowered himself to the ground. "I guess they're not going to attack today after all."

"Yes, but I dread seeing what Iturbide looks like."

"No kidding."

"Did you hear anything about how long we'll have to wait here?"

"No, but the gabachos only have another five hours of daylight to attack us. They'll let us get dinner and go to sleep I imagine. Of course – who wants to sleep? Let's grab some coffee."

The rest of the afternoon was silent, and, as predicted, at sundown the reserve line was disbanded but soldiers were told they would reform again tomorrow. The pair went first to their barracks to eat, then out to the Iturbide to see what damage had been done and how to assist.

It was dark by the time they arrived at the fort and when they got there they found everyone, barring the posted lookouts on the walls, helping to rebuild the walls.

"I think it was optimistic to expect coffee by the campfire." Garcia said flatly.

They climbed up on the parapet and started to lend a hand putting the stones back in place. There was almost no building mortar because most people in Puebla had bricked up the window and door openings. Consequently, the men were just stacking rubble in place.

It appeared to Juan Antonio and Garcia that most of the cannons had been rendered useless, although the barrels themselves were still intact. The majority of the cannons were made of Spanish bronze and had been dented, if not from shot, then from collapsing when the platform underneath sustained a direct hit. The men were extracting the barrels from the rubble and attempting to repair their mounts, but it did not look good. There was even talk of placing the barrels in piles of rock to brace them against recoil.

As the youths worked they learned that nearly every man with the courage to fire the cannons had perished under the withering onslaught; in some cases, three crews had died trying to keep the cannons firing through the course of the exchange. This saddened them, and they redoubled their efforts to rebuild the fort. Juan Antonio was handing a stone to Garcia when abruptly they heard shots.

"Alarm!" one of the sentinels cried.

"Alarm!"

All of the soldiers stopped working and reached for their rifles, scanning the darkness. Juan Antonio could perceive movement in the obscurity although it was impossible to discern any forms.

"Fuego!" commanded a Mexican voice.

One of the remaining corner cannons fired to his right, illuminating the night sky near the bastion. Along the wall, rifle fire erupted as the Mexicans leveled their rifles on the parapet and fired at the shadows. Almost immediately, flashes of return fire could be seen in the darkness, hundreds of them, a good distance out.

Juan Antonio heard a cry to his left and glanced; one of the men on the wall had taken a ball in the shoulder. Next to him Garcia was firing his pistol with deliberate care, aiming at the flashes of the enemy guns. But since Juan Antonio did not have a rifle he could only peer over the parapet. He could hear the whistling of bullets in the air although most of them overshot their targets. Then, from behind the rifle flashes, cannon fire began. Over the course of the next few minutes, cannonballs crashed into the earth, in front of the fort or into the lowest part of the wall, but a few hit higher, knocking men back and throwing debris in all directions.

Staring out, Juan Antonio could see French soldiers silhouetted by the cannon explosions; there were hundreds of them standing or kneeling, firing at the fort.

Suddenly on their left from the darkness came more shouts and firing. Turning to his side Juan Antonio saw several hundred Mexican troops, presumably from the Morelos, running diagonally across the field to a position in front of the French riflemen. What bravery!

The French diverted their fire to that group and the Mexican troops took casualties.

Juan Antonio felt a swell of rage and helplessness. If only he had a rifle he could participate! Garcia had stopped firing to keep from endangering their fellow comrades in arms on the field below.

The French artillery shifted and fired at the soldiers in the field, causing grievous losses. Juan Antonio counted at least fifteen fallen. But the counterattack appeared to have driven the French off, as the rifle flashes diminished and fell back. Having achieved this, the men of the garrison from Morelos, under heavy cannon fire, retreated back to their fort. The cannons, on the other hand, did not cease and Juan Antonio could feel the walls shaking from the impacts.

"We should get off the walls, Juan Antonio!" Garcia had grabbed Juan Antonio's arm and was almost yelling.

Juan Antonio nodded and he and Garcia turned to scamper along the parapet to the stairs. All this time the artillery of both sides had been firing at one another. Some of the men were descending but most remained peeking over the parapet, rifles at the ready.

Juan Antonio's heart raced with adrenaline and he was having trouble breathing properly.

"Hey Garcia, they didn't charge."

Garcia just stared back at him, panting heavily.

"It's just weird." Juan Antonio continued. "We spotted them and opened fire and they just fired back. It was a big group too."

"Just as well." Garcia said. "Gabachos!"

The artillery exchange went on for another hour or so. More guards were posted on the wall and the men settled back to repairing what damage they could, although there were few places where they could do this without exposing themselves to hostile fire.

Just as they were returning to work on the wall Juan Antonio said to Garcia "Officially we're off duty tomorrow."

"No such thing here."

"Well, what I'm trying to say is, why don't we sleep here in case they get attacked again? They'll need everybody they can get if the gabachos breach the wall."

"You don't think we'll get in trouble?"

"Not if we send word."

So the boys resolved to pass the night there to help protect the fort against another night raid. The remainder of the night passed uneventfully and they were awakened by a sergeant at the crack of dawn. He asked them to follow him and they were taken to Captain Ramiro in the courtyard.

The captain bade them good morning.

"Buenos días, Captain." They replied dutifully.

"I want to inform General Ortega that the western side is mostly demolished and that we are going to construct a smaller cannon platform in the courtyard so that we can fire over the remnants of the outer walls. Tell him also we repulsed an assault last night with the aid of the soldiers from Morelos and that we feel we can hold for another day or two. That is all."

The captain turned away and went to the Convent of San Javier, which was being reinforced with stones in the windows and doorways for an eventual breakthrough.

"You hombres can come back again if you want." the sergeant said. "That is, if you're foolhardy enough."

THE COURAGE IN THE HEARTS OF MEN

March 28, 1863

It was noon.

Juan Antonio and Garcia were present in the meeting hall with General Ortega, General Troncosco of Iturbide, Colonel Auza of Morelos, General Ghilardi of Hidalgo, General Rojo of Demócrata, and Quartermaster General Mendoza. Despite the fact it was a closed meeting of the western commanders, the young men had been permitted to remain at the far end of the room with the guard. General Troncosco was describing the extent of the French fieldworks.

"The French sappers have by now completed a third trench line with connecting communication trenches. We think they will continue to build a fourth trench perhaps one hundred meters from us. Thousands of enemy soldiers are in this network, crouching and digging, and the continuous artillery cover fire makes it impossible for us to fire back. Colonel Auza concurs with me that we cannot last as his own artillery, supporting us, has also been knocked out.

"Having said this, although we are depleted, we request permission to maintain our positions yet another day. Should we withdraw without a fight the French will breach our outer line without losses. The men have committed to stand."

There was a moment of weighty silence as the generals regarded one another across the center table. Over the silence, the noise of cannons carried the obvious sign of the unstoppable French advance.

Ortega spoke first. "You have completed the strengthening of the convent and the city perimeter line?"

"In the fort, yes, but I cannot speak for the city strongpoints."

"They are ready sir." It was Quartermaster General Mendoza. "All our reinforcements have been repositioned to the building line behind Iturbide. We can transfer the heavy cannons to the other forts and leave a few of the field pieces for the defense of the courtyard."

"You men are heroic, but I cannot believe this to be our best course of action." Ortega said. "The wall is almost destroyed and you will soon be overwhelmed by superior numbers. Do you really mean to stand another day?"

"Yes, my General. We have all requested your permission to hold the fort another day."

"Well, I still want the artillery transferred as well as any reserves that can be spared from our response battalion sent to the plaza line. With your courage, we will exact a heavy price for the Iturbide, but we must not delude ourselves that we can repel their attack. I grant you permission to hold the fort until further notice.

"Auza and Ghilardi, you must do what you can for the men in the Iturbide – including positioning cannons to cover the adjoining streets. If the French break through too quickly, we cannot let them flank us and cut you off.

He looked at the ranking general of the Iturbide. "Troncosco, don't keep your men in there too long. We want a heroic stand to the last minute, not a massacre."

With the decisions made, the officers took their leave of Ortega, who called the two young men over. "Hey, muchachos!"

"Sí, General?"

"If you're going to fight outside your units you will need rifles. Guard, go get them each one of the new English percussion rifles."

Juan Antonio's spirits were buoyed immediately. They were going to be issued arms by Ortega personally! To him, it represented part of a personal dream. The guard returned from the armory down the hall carrying a couple of shiny new dark rifles with bandoliers of bullets.

"See, they are this year's model. Eighteen sixty-threes; imported from England. If the norteamericanos won't sell us their Henry repeating rifles, then we can at least buy the best from the British. They come with bayonets also; I imagine you'll need them." The young men looked at the brilliant new rifles with pride.

"If I am so desperate that I must break a promise to an old friend, then at least I can prepare you adequately for what will come." Ortega continued. "You have already put in for a transfer to the Guanajuato battalions, and, I know even if I deny this, you will still go. You are patriots to the bone. I will not transfer you, but I will permit you to go and fight alongside your friends if you so choose. Just be careful and try to stay near the rear wall, will you? As a favor for a friend?"

The general was smiling as he patted Juan Antonio on the shoulder. The steady eyes of the general seemed to simultaneously express fondness and fatigue. Or was it worry?

"We will, General Ortega. Thank you so much!" Juan Antonio could barely believe his good fortune. He had been given a modern rifle by General Ortega himself!

They excused themselves and went to the barracks to collect their belongings. They would be going directly to the Iturbide.

As they walked in the direction of the cannon fire, they were passed in all directions by soldiers in a great hurry.

When they arrived at Iturbide, they found the western wall to be mostly destroyed. Only the lower half of the wall remained standing and even this was just a rounded pile of rubble. It was clear the French were obliterating this obstacle with their artillery.

The Guanajuatan soldiers had been redistributed throughout points in the interior of the fort. Cannons had been shifted to the courtyard to cover the Convent of San Javier entryway and the expanse between the walls. Soldiers inside the convent were peering over the sandbags that lined the windows and tops of partially bricked up doorways.

"We haven't even started fighting yet!" One of the cannon men said to them as they came near. "It will be different once they stop hiding behind their artillery."

In the adjacent forts of Morelos and Demócrata, the cannons had been reset to cover the streets exiting the fort in case of a breakthrough. It seemed eerie to observe the artillery pointing down the streets toward the two hundred men gathered to reinforce any faltering position. This was where they could be assigned, as they were not full infantry.

As the bombardment continued throughout the afternoon, slowly dismantling the western wall fragment by fragment, the two boys learned through conversation with their fellow soldiers, that the French had more than forty guns shooting at them. For some reason the French did not concentrate them simultaneously. The soldiers knew the intent of their enemy was to sap their morale through constant bombardment, but the effect it had was the opposite. Instead, in the interior of the fort the Mexicans tapped their fingers on their rifles, waiting for the opportunity for revenge. The reserve soldiers waited anxiously, physically at ease but mentally aware that any minute they would be in for the fight of their lives.

As nightfall came, the soldiers communicated that they were posting triple sentries and asked the reserves to be alert and prepared.

"It would be pretty cowardly of them to attack at night." Garcia said. Juan Antonio, who was settling against the inside wall of one of the buildings to sleep, agreed. Garcia sat down next to him, and they laid their rifles across their laps and closed their eyes, trying to relax.

The French had stopped their bombardment when the sun went down, but every twenty or thirty minutes they fired a shot to awaken the defenders. Most men in the group hardly slept between the expectation of an imminent attack, the discomfort, and the intermittent cannon shots. Nobody spoke yet everyone was poignantly aware of each other.

Shortly before sunrise, the captain told everyone to get up. As few had slept this was a relief and they stood right up.

"God, I slept awful" Juan Antonio muttered as he staggered to his feet.

"At least you slept." Garcia retorted.

The men assembled together in the plaza with their weapons. No one spoke, but everyone stared at the back of the convent and into the courtyard. Turning to Garcia and leaning toward him to avoid being overheard, Juan Antonio whispered, "This is when they'll hit us, at first light."

The sun rose and the walls cast shadows. Everything was dead quiet and it was then that Juan Antonio realized there was no cannon fire. He shivered abruptly from the morning chill, fatigue and tension. In the distance they heard a bird begin to chirp; then another answered. He could almost read the minds of the soldiers in the convent manning the sandbag positions, their rifles loaded and cocked, aiming straight at the west side of the fort, waiting.

Perhaps twenty minutes passed and the shadows shortened. Direct sunlight fell right on the western wall where everyone's eyes were fixed. Would they wait until full light?

"Tirez!"

The French command to shoot carried into the courtyard and then there were multiple explosions. The bombardment had recommenced.

It was as strong as the previous day's deluge and the men resigned themselves to another day of waiting in anticipation.

"I didn't know they had this many cannonballs in all of France." Garcia exclaimed wryly over the cannonade.

The bombardment was practically on top of them now, crashing into the half-standing wall in front of them. Occasionally a piece of debris would fly higher than the rest and land only yards from them in the courtyard or a lucky shot would trigger another smaller collapse of the wall.

The day dragged on painfully, and at approximately two o'clock Captain Ramiro left to attend the daily officers' briefing to learn what they would do with the exhausted reserve unit that was running on little sleep and even less food. However tired the men were, though, they knew it was only a fraction of the fatigue the Guanajuatan soldiers must be enduring. They couldn't discuss it with them as now every soldier was huddled down in cover.

The heat of the afternoon and the stress of the shelling began to take its toll on the men and Juan Antonio began to wish word would come that they would be replaced. If the French were not going to attack today, then they might not even attack tomorrow.

Then, at about four o'clock, the firing intensified.

Their captain returned, saying they had orders to stay at least until nightfall. Juan Antonio had never witnessed such furor at point-blank range as dust and smoke began to fill the courtyard. This was an ominous sign and every soldier squared himself for the impending battle. The shelling continued for some time then suddenly stopped. Within seconds, Juan Antonio heard one of the Guanajuatan men fire – then a second report. More rifles started to fire, and he saw running French soldiers in the plaza. Then the earth itself seemed to erupt into gunfire.

Some fell as they were hit but there were hundreds of them swarming over the reduced wall. He heard the Mexican cannons firing in the fort's interior and saw the Guanajuatan men in a melee with the French in the courtyard, mere yards from where they were standing. His legs felt rubbery and his heart was racing. There were so many of them!

"Charge!" the captain cried and the men surged forward. Juan Antonio sensed Garcia at his side.

The French troops were perhaps two hundred yards away on the opposite side of the courtyard and were closing fast, engaging the Guanajuatan men in hand-to-hand combat. When they were about ten paces away Juan Antonio aimed his rifle, raising it halfway to his shoulder, and slowed his step. He saw a French soldier with a red cap and loose red breeches – a Zouave! Most of the soldiers appeared to be Arab conscripts with the billowy pants and sashes. They looked fearsome and intimidating.

The Zoave was running ahead of the others toward Juan Antonio, who aimed at the enemy's midriff and pulled the trigger. The rifle kicked against his arm and Juan Antonio smelled the sulfurous odor of gunpowder. He lowered the rifle and kept running while staring at the soldier he had just shot. The man was holding his rib cage and had let his rifle drop.

They had almost reached the French troops when Juan Antonio heard the French command "Charge à baïonnette!"

The Zouaves raised their rifles and raced headlong for the Mexicans.

"Adelante!" It was Garcia.

Almost instantly the Zouaves hit them. One of them selected Juan Antonio and charged, thrusting his bayonet at Juan Antonio, who narrowly managed to parry with his rifle by using it as a club.

There was the sound of a shot right next to him and the Arab was flung backward, as if a hammer had hit him in the chest. His arms were flung forward, and his face was contorted in an expression of pained shock. He did not get up. Turning, Juan Antonio saw Garcia there next to him chasing another Arab with his bayonet.

He scanned for an unengaged Zouave at close range to fight. They seemed to be everywhere and the only thing he could be certain of in the fracas was that they were badly outnumbered.

He heard someone begin to scream on his left. He turned his head just in time to see a bearded Zouave charging him with his rifle lowered and pointed straight at him, a curved bayonet fixed to the front. The rifle fired and Juan Antonio felt a sting in his left side. His vision blurred for a split second but the Zouave was still coming at him and Juan Antonio cleared his head, and lowered his bayonet in front of him to brace for the thrust. The Arab knocked Juan Antonio's rifle to the side and tried to bring his bayonet up to stab Juan Antonio in the face. He was too close for this and just tapped Juan Antonio's head. Juan Antonio butted him in the stomach with the base of his rifle, but the Zouave seemed unfazed. Their rifles and arms locked and in a test of strength, each man trying to overbear the other by pushing forward with his rifle. But, the Zouave was taller than Juan Antonio and he had to take a step backwards.

They grappled like this for some instants before Juan Antonio remembered his knife. Pushing himself in closer to the soldier and hooking the tip of his rifle over the edge of the Zouave's, Juan Antonio reached for his knife with his left hand. Then his opponent smacked him on the face with the barrel of his rifle and Juan Antonio saw stars for a moment.

With this advantage, the Zouave attempted to push his rifle in front of Juan Antonio's arm but to no avail. Juan Antonio squirmed and plunged the knife into the man's kidney. The Arab jumped forward and his expression changed from rage to shock. Their eyes met and Juan Antonio thought he had never seen a man look so surprised in his life. He pushed the knife in farther and pressed his chest against the Zouave, whose strength was ebbing. His hand felt warm and wet from the man's blood.

Their eyes were locked and the Arab's expression changed back to anger as his eyes narrowed. He tried to extract his rifle from Juan Antonio's entangling grip but Juan Antonio held on. Finally, Juan Antonio withdrew his knife and the man gasped. It was then Juan Antonio noticed how strange the soldier's cap was. It hung down the nape of his neck like a stocking. The man's mouth hung open and he was muttering something in a very raspy language; Arabic?

From somewhere someone cried in Spanish "Retreat! Retreat!"

Juan Antonio broke his stare from the dying Zouave and examined his surroundings. He could hardly see any Mexicans and he seemed to be drowning in a sea of Arab uniforms and the blue jackets of the Frenchmen. He cast one last glance at the man he had stabbed. The Zouave was trying to sit down but was doubled over, with one hand clutching his wound and the other propping his body up.

With that, Juan Antonio began to run toward the retreating Mexicans. Some sort of wound in his left abdomen throbbed as he ran but it did not seem serious.

The Mexicans were running back behind the Convent San Javier when some of them spun, formed a loose firing line, and fired a volley at the French forces. Juan Antonio was in front of them, but miraculously was not hit. He did hear the thud of the bullets hitting the bodies of the enemy and abruptly his thoughts went to Garcia, who he had not seen since he had saved his life.

He reached the men and turned to face the oncoming French, who had stopped to regroup and absorb reinforcements. There were hundreds inside the walls now; most of them were starting to force their way into the convent through the scant entrances, but some had dropped to their knees and were firing on his group. Juan Antonio had not even realized they were under fire, but when he scanned around him he saw many of his comrades had fallen in the courtyard or on the makeshift firing line. Juan Antonio felt a pang of regret that he had not grabbed the weapon of the Zouave he had slain.

He joined his fellow soldiers in firing at the mass of soldiers confronting them and for a brief period the two groups exchanged waves of metal. On the French side, you almost couldn't miss because there were so many in such a small area and reinforcements were moving up behind them to catch stray shots. He confirmed wounding at least one more gabacho; a Frenchman with a blue jacket and tall leather boots. But, the Mexicans were absorbing horrific casualties too and Juan Antonio saw out of the corner of his eye that their line was starting to crack.

As he turned to run with the rest of the line, he felt fortunate not to be in the rear this time. Nevertheless, as he ran he heard and felt the jar of a ball deflect off the barrel of his rifle. And, he still could not locate Garcia.

The men ran through the archway that split the courtyard and were temporarily safe from the hail of French bullets. The group ran to the middle of the court and wheeled to face the direction they'd come from. Through the arch, they could see the soldiers moving toward them. Behind them were the streets of the city. Reloading as quickly as they could, they leveled their rifles.

Then, they saw the mass of French soldiers, for some reason, halt and divert their attention upwards. Juan Antonio heard a cannon shot from higher up in the fort, or perhaps on the stairs of the wall. Somebody must have a cannon up there, firing on the French in the courtyard!

He could see the enemy troops crouch, then run to the northeast corner of the wall. Even though he could only glimpse a small portion of the fighting he watched the French run at the wall three times, each time falling back then being driven forward by new reinforcements. The cannon fire seemed extremely rapid despite the fact it was a sole cannon. For the time being their group was ignored by the French.

As they looked out the arch, dozens of Guanajuatan men began to stagger through to their side of the courtyard. These were the men who had been in the San Javier convent. Simultaneously, Juan Antonio heard another cannon open fire on the south side of the courtyard although it was impossible to determine if it the Mexicans or the French firing a captured field piece.

Juan Antonio saw the Guanajuatan soldiers who had fallen back from the convent stop when they reached the volunteer's line and started to talk, motioning with their hands and regrouping. By now the group numbered in the hundreds and Juan Antonio saw Lieutenant Colonel Fernandez gesturing for the men to reform into their units.

He also perceived that the sound of the lone cannon from the other side of the patio had now ceased, and had been replaced by cannon fire around the fort on all sides.

The lieutenant colonel raised his pistol in the air and, swinging it down, gave them the order to counterattack. The men ran forward, hundreds of them, Juan Antonio with them, emboldened and reinvigorated. The rush of the initial breakthrough had subsided and now he felt very angry at the indignity of being dislodged from the main part of the fort.

He watched the leading men in the group go through the arch and heard an incredible amount of rifle fire from in front of them. Caught in the press, he charged back through the arch into the main courtyard and straight into the inferno. Before him the courtyard was filled with smoke and strewn with dead bodies – Mexican, Arab, French.

The ground was littered with rubble and fragments of wood from the walls of San Javier convent and facing them were scores of French and Zouaves with their rifles pointed at the archway. They were running headfirst into a storm of bullets!

All around him his fellow soldiers were grasping their bodies after being hit by a ball or falling forward, struck dead instantly. Juan Antonio charged forward and blindly discharged his rifle from his hip into the group before him.

His eyes were starting to smart from the gun smoke and every step forward he took, there seemed to be fewer Mexicans with him. As the ranks in front were thinning, he felt his courage and battle rage begin to fade. Suddenly, as if the men ahead of him had read his mind, they turned around and began to flee back to the archway. They were retreating!

He hesitated and stared at his comrades running toward him. Their eyes were fixed on a point beyond him and filled with fright. As he watched, several more fell, shot in the back.

The enemy fire persisted and with that, Juan Antonio turned and ran back. The group had nearly completely turned around, and the men practically dived back through the archway, but not before many had died trying to reach it.

Somehow he made it back through and followed the rest of the men out of the fort. The lieutenant colonel was nowhere in sight and panic reined. The men scattered into the buildings on the fringe of the city and he ran with them.

Casting a glance behind him he saw other troops moving in to cover their backs. With a start, he realized he had no idea of Garcia's whereabouts. God forbid he should have perished back there, or worse fallen wounded and abandoned by him! He would never forgive himself for breaking his oath.

Thinking of Garcia, he slowed and came to a halt, and searching for his friend's face amongst the soldiers that hurtled past him. He couldn't locate Garcia, so he ran also until they all reached a church plaza where they stopped to recover.

It was perhaps five thirty.

TRIAL OF MANHOOD

March 29, 1863

All around the plaza exhausted soldiers were leaning on their rifles, catching their breath, or sitting with their backs against a wall. Some had discarded their weapons to run faster and Juan Antonio was happy he had retained his. A surge of pride ran through him. After months of self-doubt and uncertainty, he had proven to himself that he was courageous and would not falter in the face of the enemy! This had been his first time truly on the front line, not under the tutelage of General Ortega, and he had fought well. Accompanying the sensation of pride came a feeling of relief. For months he had built this moment up as his trial of manhood, and he had passed. Despite the fact they retreated and most likely lost the fort of Iturbide, Juan Antonio still felt elated.

Still, he had not found Garcia and the stragglers appeared to be tapering off. He had verified all the faces in the plaza. Asking some of the later arrivals if there were more on their way, he learned that a small group had rallied when they saw the reinforcements protecting their retreat.

Maybe Garcia had elected to stay with them.

He stayed just a little while longer to drink some water and wash the bullet graze on his left side. Miraculously the Arab's bullet had hardly skimmed his left abdomen, just enough to take off some flesh and make him wince when the adrenaline faded. Carrying a canteen with him, he began to retrace the steps of their retreat back toward the Iturbide. He had not paid much attention to the buildings on the route before, but now they seemed to loom over his head and filled him with a mild sense of rebuke and shame.

The sun was dropping in the sky and soon the buildings would cast shadows. It was now maybe six o'clock, and he figured if they could hold until nightfall, the French would never attack at night and they could regroup.

"Juan Antonio!" came a cry from one of the buildings.

Scanning the street he saw Garcia motioning to him from one of the window openings nearby. It was not bricked up and Garcia had leaned out and was gesturing for him to come in.

"Hola! Voy!" Juan Antonio yelled excitedly.

He entered the building and saw five or six men, only one in uniform, with Garcia. They all looked haggard and on edge but ready to fight again. Two had rifles and the rest, including Garcia, had only pistols.

Looking out the back of the small two-room house he saw that the rear of the building stood on a plaza across which they could see the walls of the Iturbide. These men must have stopped on the fringes of town and had not run all the way.

"You made it!" said Garcia, grinning broadly and clasping Juan Antonio's hand.

"And you also. We got separated –"

"Yes, but that it won't happen again. And it's irrelevant because neither one of us died! We didn't break our vow."

The other men had already lost interest in them and were staring out the rear of the house, weapons ready.

"I stopped when I saw these men," Garcia continued, "we're hiding here in case the French try to push ahead before nighttime. More deployed behind us as we fled so we should be all right unless the gabachos get ambitious. So, what happened to you?"

"Oh, I was okay. I killed four or five gabachos, well – maybe only a couple – but I stabbed a Zouave right up close. He'd shot me."

"He shot you?" Garcia interjected.

"Yes, right here." Juan Antonio touched the bullet graze on his side. "It's not bad really. I only notice it when I'm resting."

"Well you must sit down. Come on."

Garcia led him into the back room facing the plaza and sat him down against the wall. They continued to relate their personal tales from the day. Both young men had fought valiantly and were proud of themselves. Garcia had lost his rifle when it was emptied and he'd had to cast it away to wrestle with a Frenchman.

The other soldiers listened with half an ear while they stared out the partially bricked up windows. Each man seemed lost in his own world, or recuperating for the next battle.

They didn't talk for long as within twenty minutes or so, the artillery fire started again. It mounted very quickly and within several minutes the inferno had returned. This was even louder than they had heard in the Iturbide and seemed to come from all around them. There were so many guns firing that individual shots could not be discerned and the noise was deafening. Cannonballs from the French side started falling in the plaza and striking the surrounding buildings. It looked like the French would attack after all. A ball impacted right in front of their building and smoke and debris flew into the interior of the house. For some moments there was no visibility and the men began to cough violently. The air was thick with dust and Juan Antonio had trouble breathing. They were going to get hit again. He needed to prepare.

Standing up as the dust settled, Juan Antonio headed over to the windows, picking up his rifle. Just then there was a loud explosion and he caught a glimpse of bricks flying away from the window toward him.

Everything went black.

AN ENTIRE NATION IN THE BALANCE

April 1, 1863

It was nighttime and Presidente Benito Juárez stood staring out his balcony window. It had been some time since he had received news of the siege of Puebla but travelers and stragglers brought word that the city still stood despite the French encirclement and bombardments.

Here in the capital the government was protected by General Comonfort and ten thousand older soldiers. Would it be the correct decision to send them to try to free the besieged defenders? To do so would leave the rest of the country defenseless, and if the French were to outflank or rout the Army of the Center... General Comonfort seemed to prefer the parade grounds and endless meetings in full regalia to the blood of the battlefield. To think he had been obliged to grant control of the Army of the Center to a man who had once thrown him in prison in a move to retain dictatorial control. Such was the state of his beloved nation. Alas! And their northern neighbors continued distracted, torn apart by their own conflict. Just today the United States government had authorized conscription of soldiers. The end of their war was nowhere in sight.

México, God bless her, under sky and sea, could never hope to beat the French in an open fight. Their only salvation lay in the support of the United States, the Union, and intervention against their mutual enemy, the French, who supplied and supported the Confederate rebels and conspired to establish a colony right under their noses! México must hold out until the norteamericanos could back them. For once Mexico could be thankful for the Monroe Doctrine and norteamericano vision of caretaker of the Americas. The French were stopped at Puebla. If Puebla should fall, México would fall.

Presidente Juárez cast a final look at the streets of the capital. Moonlight was reflecting off the paving stones and white washed walls of the buildings. Everything was tranquil, an illusion of peace and serenity. It was hard to believe they were on the verge of collapse.

God be with the men at Puebla.

RECUPERATING

April 3, 1863

Juan Antonio feebly opened his eyes. It was daytime and there was a good deal of sunlight in the room. He was prone on the ground, covered in blankets. His head throbbed. He remembered he had come to, once, the previous night. It seemed ages ago. What day was it?

He opened his eyes again, but the glare made him wince immediately. Something was constricting his head; bandages he assumed. There were three windows on the opposite wall, and he and roughly twenty other men were lying on the floor on sheets. Obviously a recovery ward. His side felt fine, and was also wrapped in cloth, but his head was killing him!

The last thing he remembered was the wall exploding before him… what had happened to Garcia? Had he survived the blast? And how was the battle going? He needed to know so much and he couldn't see anyone who seemed to be supervising them.

Some of the men were conscious and, when he lifted his head, they made eye contact with him, but nobody exerted himself to greet him.

He noticed there was a tin cup with water and some stale bread on a plate next to his space. Food was the last thing on his mind, but he was unbearably thirsty and reached for the cup. Searing pains hit his head like a hammer and he saw grey spots for a moment, but despite the discomfort he slowly extended his hand and lifted the cup to his lips. Lowering it back to the floor gently, he whispered to his closest neighbor "Hey, what day is it?"

"No sé." the wounded man replied gruffly. It looked like he had been injured in the torso or shoulder, because the left side of his upper body was heavily bandaged.

"What's happening in the battle?" Juan Antonio pressed.

"No sé."

It seemed he would have to wait for the answers to his questions. Juan Antonio closed his eyes and attempted to relax despite the throbbing of his head. The best he could hope for was a quick recovery from his head injury. He wasn't sure which ached more, his head or his heart. Not knowing what was happening and concern over the fate of Garcia plagued him. He slipped into a semi-comatose state again.

The following day Garcia came to visit him it was early evening. Juan Antonio was dozing at the time. A doctor had come through twice to check on the patients during the day. He had only been able to tell him what he already knew – that he had sustained a severe blow to his head and that he needed rest.

He awoke to Garcia tapping his shoulder.

"Feeling better?" Garcia inquired.

"Ahhh…" Juan Antonio murmured, propping himself on his elbow and trying to ignore the thunderbolts of pain that racked his head.

"I guess not," Garcia said. "You got hit pretty hard. Of course, you can't slouch around here forever. You'll miss all the fun!"

"What day is it?"

"April fourth. You've been out for six days, mi hermano."

"And what's happening?"

"A lot. The French are really hitting us hard now, since yesterday. That's why I haven't been able to come by more often. We're fighting house by house, manzana by manzana, by bayonet lots of the time. For a couple of days they tore up the city with their cannons; you should see where you were when you took the blow. You wouldn't recognize it. All the buildings are in ruins. But even the French don't have enough ammunition to demolish every building in the city, so they have to come close and that's when we get them."

"What happened to me?"

"You got hit by a brick. When the cannonball hit the wall, the wall didn't hold and the bricks flew everywhere. It was actually safer up close to the windows. We all got knocked down and one of the men got a glancing blow to the chin, but you got smacked right on the head. I brought you back here. It was no problem, they didn't attack us that night."

"What has the fighting been like?"

"Hectic. Deadly. Lots of dead on both sides. The French always send the Zuaves in first, and they seem to hate us. At the range between buildings we have no warning either, they just suddenly charge out of the buildings across the street by the hundreds. But you know, you're not the only one who's killed a man mano-a-mano now."

"That seems like another lifetime."

"Yes, me too. I guess that's good. This war is so cruel it's better to wake up each morning like a man reborn and try to put your guilt and sins to rest. "

They became quiet and then Garcia picked up the tin cup and went out of the building to a nearby well. He returned with the full cup and put it down next to Juan Antonio.

"There have been two big battles; Guadalupita and Hospicio. Both finished with hand-to-hand. The French used sappers and artillery to destroy the walls that we were posted behind, then they came at us. You know General Porfirio Díaz? He heroically defended a cannon and its last operator by fighting with a pistol butt. They say he's unstoppable. He drove the French back last night."

"How's General Ortega?"

"Fine I guess. Well, probably concerned." Garcia said, smiling. "I should go, there's bound to be more fighting soon. You rest up and get better."

"Okay, take care of yourself. Bring me more news soon!"

"Hasta luego."

And with that Juan Antonio lay back down gently and reflected on the situation.

THE BEST LAID PLANS...

April 8, 1863

Louis-Napoléon reined in his steed and drew to a halt. The ride through the forest of Fontainebleau had cleared his head. The latest news from Mexico was frustrating as always; the tenacious resistance at Puebla, heavy losses in the army, talk of bypassing Puebla and dashing to Mexico City en masse… Tempting as this was, they could never let the Mexicans beat them at Puebla a second time, otherwise every half-wit in the Empire would get the idea to barricade themselves in a fort and wait out the French army. No, Puebla would have to be reduced, house by house!

There had even been rumors of a request to dismantle the naval guns from the ships in Veracruz and haul them inland, or to transport artillery from the colonies in the Antilles! What a nuisance this ardent Mexican patriotism was turning out to be! They were stalling everything.

At Miramar the Archduke Maximilian awaited complete preparation of Mexico for his puppet regime and in North America the Confederates cried for French support on their southern flank. All of this was being delayed by peasants with machetes!

He sighed and regarded the profile of the Château of Fontainebleau with its multiple-level roofs which were accentuated by dozens of chimneys of varying heights. He could understand why this château had been the countryside favorite of the rulers of France for centuries. Why, his own uncle had departed for Elba Island from this very palace in 1814, only to return from exile in arms shortly afterward.

Ah, to be a great emperor like his uncle… but these were troubled times; Prussia on the east, England across the Channel, Garibaldi and his nationalists in the Italian peninsula threatening the Pope in Rome. The French were not what they used to be either; his uncle had inherited the force and anger of a people hardened by over a decade of revolutionary violence and his control of the press had been absolute. And across the Atlantic the power of the United States had grown, unchecked by any close rival. The schism in the United States was essential to the continuation of European hegemony in the world.

He smelled the scent of lamb drifting from one of the countless chimneys and thought of dinner that evening. It would be their first dinner on the new porcelain from Sèvres. It was decorated in pastoral scenes with full-color inlays on the plates and bowls, a radical departure from the classic Imperial China patterns that were à la mode. There were new electroplated silver pieces from Christofle as well.

Spurring his horse toward the château he permitted himself one closing thought on Mexico.

"I'll squeeze them dry for this."

THE RUINS OF PUEBLA

April 16, 1863

Juan Antonio was walking along a street strewn with rubble. The broad avenue was flanked by two-story stores and houses in unbroken rows on either side but some of them had been riddled by cannonades and you could see right through to the other side. Almost two weeks had passed and Juan Antonio had nearly recovered. The blow to his head ached periodically but his bullet scrape had healed and he walked steadily now. But despite the fact that he had effectively recuperated as of a few days ago, General Ortega demanded he take a less active role. He had spent the recent days assisting in the ceaseless task of fortifying building lines and plazas, or delivering supplies.

The French had been inactive for some time; there had been further assaults the week before but they had been repulsed at grievous losses to the French and their Arab conscripts. They were reinforcing their army with reinforcements from Orizaba and munitions sent from France. While they had been stopped at a fortified line of buildings in the west, they were increasing their bombardment of the southern forts of Hidalgo and Ingenhieros.

Garcia on the other hand still stood guard in the west side of the city, staring at the French positions over mostly bricked up windows. Ammunition was running low so it was a miracle that the French delayed their campaign. Their only hope would be to outlast the French or hang on until the winter. Possibly by the wintertime the norteamericanos would have ended their war and would drive the French out of México. Of course, food was scarce, so they didn't have a solution for how to last until winter, even if they could.

Juan Antonio looked at the buildings around him. In most cases all that remained was the exterior shell. The interior walls had collapsed. Puebla had become a ghost town of fortified shells whose structures' only purpose now was to conceal soldiers. The sun shone uninhibited into the interiors because nearly all of the roofs had caved in. The building walls were pockmarked by bullet holes and cannonball strikes.

On the sides facing the French, any street level windows and doors had been bricked up or blocked by sandbags with just enough space for one to fire over them. Juan Antonio mused how the soldiers had also become shells; hungry, low on ammunition, and battered by enemy fire. But, like the buildings, they still stood and the French would have to knock them down, man by man.

Juan Antonio located the buildings where Garcia was posted on the western side. He entered through the destroyed rear wall of a building and saw Garcia leaning with his back against a wall with his eyes shut. He looked whipped. There were maybe a dozen other soldiers there in the skeleton of the building.

The days were hotter now and the sun beat down on everyone inside, sapping their energy. Juan Antonio waved to the other men and lowered himself down next to his friend. Garcia didn't stir so he patted him gently on the knees.

"Hey... always taking siestas."

Awaking, Garcia replied after a brief hesitation, "That's me. What are you doing here?"

"I got tired of waiting around to deliver supplies when there are none. I've spent the last few days stacking rubble and bricks back in place. I needed a break. Still quiet up here? You have it easy, I tell you."

"Pretty much. They keep us guessing. We know most of them are in the south now, but they shoot at us every once in a while and attack a house or two to keep us pinned down. We know they're not serious and only fire when they try to take our positions. As we're low on ammunition that's all we can do. No one even thinks of attacking."

"Have you heard anything about reinforcements or food?" Juan Antonio said.

"I was going to ask you the same thing! You're the one back with the generals! There's talk that we might try to break out to save the Army of the East. We could link up with the Army of the Center and defend the capital. Some of the generals are going to mention it to General Ortega, or at least that's what we hear."

"He'll never do it. I heard him saying that this battle was more important than even the Army of the East. He said it had become a question of national pride before the whole world. He says everyone in Europe is watching us in disbelief as we hold back the French. They're in shock."

"Yes, but it's only April. There's no way we'll last another six months like this." Garcia wiped his brow. "It's hardly even been one month. We can't hold on without reinforcements and supplies, try as we might. This morning I saw some of the remaining townspeople wandering in the French section scavenging for food. Can you believe it? They could be shot at any time by the gabachos! And they're so desperate for food they're past caring."

"Madre de Dios…" Juan Antonio exclaimed.

"Yes." Garcia stood up slowly and Juan Antonio followed suit. "I detest the French but they'll outlast us at this rate. We can't attack without ammunition and they won't have to attack us if we starve." Walking over to the window he pointed at the far side. "Look over there but don't stick your head out."

Juan Antonio stood on his toes and looked out. The street was abandoned but the buildings across the street were filled with the enemy. He could just discern the tops of their caps over the brick. He stepped back and looked at Garcia. "They have gaps in the brick. They're watching us through them."

"Yes, they use them to fire out but I don't even know if they aim when they shoot at us. It's just to make noise and keep us tense."

"They're out there waiting."

Garcia didn't reply.

"Well, I'd better get back. I should do some more construction work, I'm not crippled."

"All right. Keep your head down."

"You too. Vaya con Dios."

STARVATION

April 30, 1863

The weeks passed uneventfully and Juan Antonio recuperated. Starvation was the only weapon the French were using now. It was the end of April and for days there had been no enemy activity except for a cannon shot somewhere into the city every half hour or so to break the silence.

The idea of a breakout from the city, executed in two groups, had been considered but abandoned due to the debilitated state of the men and the strength of the French in their trench work. The food and gunpowder stores were nearly empty and hunger dominated everyone's minds. They could think of nothing else.

Morale had been boosted by a letter sent to Ortega from the French general Forey, personally imploring them to withdraw from the city to spare their lives and further devastation to the city of Puebla.

Even Forey had admitted the Mexicans had surpassed the call of duty and valor in their tenacious defense of the town. Ortega refused to surrender as long as some glimmer of hope for relief existed and he had written a communiqué to General Comonfort entreating him to come to their rescue, to launch a diversionary attack that would enable a breakout. This had been smuggled out of the city on April 29th. Now they awaited signs of relief from Comonfort's Army of the Center.

The soldiers were desperate, yet not one single individual would surrender until death by starvation was the only other option.

THE OLD SOLDIER CAPITULATES

May 16, 1863

"Come, amigo, enter." General Ortega morosely summoned Juan Antonio into the room.

"I wanted to talk with you. I don't know if I will ever see you again and I wanted to say good-bye. As you know, tomorrow we will be surrendering. We will disband our units and abandon the city. All officers will deliver themselves unarmed to the French in the Palacio del Gobierno after we have sabotaged our armament. White flags will go up at all the forts and strongpoints at five thirty tomorrow morning."

Weeks of fatigue and frustration welled up inside Juan Antonio and he began to tear silently. His head swam with emotions – that all their efforts should have been in vain!

"Don't be sad." Ortega said. "Don't be. What we have achieved will enter into history. The entire world watched México hold fast against the French army. What's more, México saw herself stand up to the French and give as good as she got. Alas, it was always going to end like this. We must be proud."

"But General, the Army of the Center did not come?"

"No. No, after their rout over a week ago, they have fled back to México City. General Comonfort has not even returned my communications. I had to learn of his defeat from the French and confirm it with our scouts. We have no more ammunition and no more food. We are going to spike the cannons and let the soldiers leave. The officers shall surrender to the French. I had tried to negotiate more favorable terms but as you know, we do not hold the cards."

"What shall I do?" Juan Antonio's bitter tears had stopped yet the despair remained.

"As your heart dictates."

"I don't know what my heart dictates." Juan Antonio replied.

"Go now. Find Garcia, wreck your weapon and prepare to leave." Ortega took his right hand in both of his and squeezed it. "Tell your father he will always be my friend and never forget why we stood here. The battle may be lost, but the war has just begun."

Tears welled up again in Juan Antonio's eyes once more and he could not maintain eye contact with the general. He turned and left, burdened by deep sorrow.

After Juan Antonio had departed, Ortega turned back to his desk. It was almost midnight. He must now write the most painful letter of his life. He knew what he had to say, yet one's pride is often one's most formidable obstacle. Several hours passed and he paced the room with an air of resignation. At around three in the morning he sat down and began to write.

"Dear General,

Being unable to defend this plaza for want of ammunition and provisions I have dissolved the army under my command and destroyed the weapons, including spiking the cannons.

As such, the plaza is under Your Excellency's control, and you may occupy it at your discretion, taking, as you deem prudent, the necessary means to avoid the evils that accompany a violent occupation when such methods are no longer required.

The generals and officers of this army will wait for you in the Palacio del Gobierno to surrender as your prisoners. I cannot, Esteemed General, continue defending this plaza anymore. If I could, do not doubt that I would. Accept, Your Excellency, my most respectful regards on this occasion."

General Jesús González Ortega

It was done. He handed it to the sentry and gave commands for it to be sent to the French general. A tremendous burden seemed lifted from his soul. In a matter of hours, he would be a French prisoner.

THE GOVERNMENT IN FLIGHT

May 31, 1863

"Señor Presidente, we leave for San Luis Potosí in ten minutes."

Juárez nodded at the aide who had jutted his head through the door and spoken to him. He looked around his office thoughtfully; half of the furniture had been packed or sold and all of his documents were in boxes on the stagecoach convoy waiting outside the Palacio del Gobierno.

Puebla had fallen to the French two weeks ago to the day. French vanguard forces were expected to reach the capital in another couple of days. The government was relocating to San Luis Potosí and would coordinate the struggle from there. It was no longer possible to hold the capital.

The French general Forey had formally accepted the surrender of the Army of the East in the center of Puebla, the French forces parading into the ruined city as victors on horseback, the Mexican officers waiting for them on foot and disarmed.

The Army of the Center had been routed by this same Forey who had humiliated the inept and spineless General Comonfort. Both armies had disintegrated and needed time to reform in the north. With a little luck they could field twenty thousand soldiers, but who could lead them? What he wouldn't give for a hundred, or even fifty, trained, trustworthy leaders!

Soon the French would enter the city and establish their satellite government. This amounted to nothing short of colonization and México would never rest until every cursed gabacho had gone back to France!

Already Forey had decreed that any citizen aiding and abetting guerrillas would be in a state of war against France and would be punished accordingly. Tales of summary executions were increasing daily.

In Europe and in the United States the invasion was condemned, yet none acted. The Union had been recently defeated at Chancellorsville, and the Confederates were only emboldened by the anticipated birth of an ally to the south, in México.

México would never stop fighting, not as long as his lungs drew breath!

From San Luis Potosí they would issue a call for resistance, and the people would never submit to French rule. When the French marched on San Luis Potosí, the government would flee to Saltillo and beyond. The French did not understand the feelings of a people who had savored the first taste of freedom in recent memory after centuries of domination only to have it removed by another foreign conqueror. The Mexicans had paid too dearly, both in recent times and before, to ever be beaten by a foppish monarch like Napoléon III. They would outlast the French.

With a wistful sigh, Presidente Juárez walked into the empty hallway, through the courtyard, and out into the street where his stagecoach awaited him.

THE CONFEDERATES IN EUROPE

July 13, 1863

Commander James Dunwoody Bulloch, Confederate naval agent, turned down the small alleyway as directed on the map he had. The alleyway ended at a small windowless door that did not have a handle. He threw a glance to his rear; the street was empty.

It was a beautiful sunny day, typical of southwestern France in this season. Bulloch was much happier here in Bordeaux than in Liverpool. Besides the pleasant weather, the French were more amenable to deal with and required less discretion. Liverpool had become his home away from home after being sent to Europe to purchase ships clandestinely on behalf of the Confederate States of America. Already he had acquired, on behalf of the Confederacy, multiple frigate raiders that terrorized Northern trade vessels and whalers.

Bulloch reached the end of the alleyway and tapped on the door with the metal handgrip of his walking stick. The door was opened instantly by a petite maid. She looked furtively up the alley, and then ushered him in.

He found himself in a small back hallway with pastel blue wallpaper decorated with white fleur-de-lis patterning. There was a window at the far end of the hall that had drawn lace curtains. The maid took his hat and opened a door midway down the hall. Taking one last moment to smooth his beard with his hand, he stepped through the door.

"Welcome Monsieur Bulloch, welcome." It was Lucian Arman, the leading shipbuilder in Bordeaux and personal associate of the French minister of state and Emperor Napoléon III.

"Good to see you, Monsieur Arman." Bulloch replied.

"You had a nice trip, yes?" Arman was not quite fluent in English.

"Yes, most pleasant, most pleasant. The journey from Paris was quite enjoyable. I do declare, you have beautiful countryside." Bulloch spoke with a relaxed Southern drawl.

"But of course. We say it is the best for wine and painting."

Both men laughed and Arman gestured for Bulloch to take a seat.

The room was modest and there was only one window, so it was a little dim. The lower half of the window was blocked by a blind so once they sat down they would not been seen from outside. The décor was frugal; there was a sofa with a small wooden table in front of it and a chair at either end of the table. The men sat facing one another in these chairs, while by the window was a plush smoking chair with an ashtray stand adjacent to it.

"I begin then?" Arman asked.

Bulloch nodded his assent.

"So, the wooden corvettes are proceeding as we plan. Two are in Nantes, two here in the docks. We put on them soon six-inch cannons. They will be fast but they will not beat the, how do you say, moniteurs?"

"Actually one would say "monitors". Your news heartens me, as the damn Yankee blockade is strangling us. It does appear they intend to divide us; Richmond had guessed this for some time. Why now, we don't know what to do a't'all."

Bulloch leaned forward anxiously in his seat. "With your permission, Monsieur Arman, as concerns the Yankee monitors, the Confederacy has decided that we must buy the two ironclads being built for His Highness the Emperor now, the *Sphinx* and the *Cheops*. Of course, you can rest assured that money is no object in this matter, and we beseech you to consider that the ironclads, while essential to the future of the Confederacy, are not as critical, if I may permit myself, to the future of the Second Empire.

"Your, ahhh… complexities in Mexico are confined completely to land and, begging your good nature and gentlemanly understanding again, the addition of a couple of ironclads to His Highness's navy will not influence that campaign. I take great liberty, my dear sir." Bulloch had a habit of arching his eyebrows as he smoothed over his dialogue with niceties and flattery.

"That is true, Monsieur Bulloch. But, we in France have worries too. Iron, we have not so much. In fact, we are late and must wait for building because of this. And our navy is necessary to counterbalance les Anglais and our aspiring neighbor to the east, Prussia. There is talk of war between Prussia and Denmark, you know. That von Bismarck… but I digress. Of course, I have discussed with His Highness your offer."

He stopped speaking, clapped his hands, and called "Jocelyn, viens vite!"

There was a pause, and the two men regarded one another with expectation. Then the maid opened the door and Monsieur Arman spoke to her in French and she left again.

"We in France desire to see the peculiar institution of the South vital and independent." Arman said once the maid was gone. "We hope to have a new partner in commerce and world matters. The

Emperor favors the Confederacy – but this you know. Part of the Confederacy was French until six decades ago."

"Why of course Monsieur Arman," Bulloch interjected eagerly "I myself worked out of New Orleans and have used on various occasions their currency – "the Dix" named for the word for ten in your language. Why, the term "Dixie" stuck and now southerners call that land Dixieland."

This elicited a condescending smile from Arman.

Bulloch pressed. "Frankly Monsieur Arman, you know the English. They want to sit on the fence and have their fingers in both pies. This won't do a't'all."

"But of course. Les Anglais are, above all, a nation of merchants. What news of our blanket company, Bravay and Compagnie? Will Laird be able to sell the rams?"

"Yes, well, rightly so. A just question." Bulloch cleared his throat. "I don't believe so. Despite the kind assistance your government – composed of men of most honorable character, I might add, has provided in having the front company acquire the boats on behalf of your government for the Pasha of Egypt, I don't think the British government has the stomach it see it through.

"John Laird has been most cooperative, of course. A right fine gentleman, I might add. It was he who built the *Alabama* and *Florida* for us, and all we did last time was sail the ships to the Bahamas under the Union Flag and arm them there. And as you know, we changed the boats' names to *El Tousson* and *El Mounassir,* but the Yankee government has spies everywhere and it would seem that Queen Victoria does prefers them. I reckon we may not receive the boats a't'all."

"Well, Monsieur Bulloch. Any ship built by France can be sailed to Mexico under the Tricolore and then north from Veracruz under the Confederate flag." Arman turned to the door and said "Tiens, rammenes-le."

Bulloch had not heard the maid reenter the room, and she approached the table now, placed some documents on it, and excused herself.

"So I discussed with His Highness Emperor Louis-Napoléon your proposal sent before," Arman said "That is to say, buy the two ironclads I build for the French navy. With eyes on our friendship, he agreed. But, we consult with the firm of Emile Erlanger, in Paris, and the value of the Confederate cotton bonds here in Europe is, how do you say, reduced? They counsel us that, with the blockade stopping cotton exportation it is not evident to get cotton and, by consequence, your bonds are worth little. Besides, les Anglais have stopped buying most of your cotton and get it now from India."

Arman handed the contract to Bulloch and continued. "The Emperor agrees, but in such a way that there is a financial compensation for the risk, and not what your government proposes. This is non-negotiable."

Bulloch started to read the contract but didn't wish to wait any longer and flipped to the back page. Good God! Much higher indeed! His head swam. This was pure profiteering; unadulterated skullduggery! Half again the real value of the ships!

In an open market this would never stand but who else would sell the Confederacy ships? He reckoned they knew the English had gotten cold feet and this was not a transitory phase. He would never hear the end of it from Richmond! And without ships to break the Yankee blockade, the Confederacy's economy would grind to a halt. He knew he had no alternative but to accept but the least he could do was confirm that the conditions of sale were in order.

"With the Laird rams," Arman said, "we will support you with the trompe d'oeuil, as we say in French. If the ships sail from Liverpool to the Pasha of Egypt, we divert them and change flags. The ships would rendezvous with a vessel of the Canal Compagnie, which is building the Suez Canal, and they can arm in the Mediterranean. The Pasha is most agreeable to us as we build the canal and founded the Service d'Antiquities Egyptienne to stop their theft of Egyptian artifacts. It will be arranged in a supple manner."

Bulloch was listening with one ear while he scanned the contract. Most everything seemed in order, apart from the ridiculous price. Delivery conditions, as Lucien Arman was describing, were flexible although he didn't see any clauses for guarantees of quality or return.

"To your south, in Mexico, we install, how do you say, a most friendly government. Just three days ago – and I tell you this in confidence, Monsieur Bulloch, because news has not yet reached general France. I know as the date was organized with the Emperor. The Mexican National Assembly voted for a Catholic and hereditary monarch to be emperor of Mexico. They vote for Ferdinand Maximilian, Archduke of Austria-Hungary. Most convenient for you, non? In case of refusal, His Highness Napoléon can choose the emperor of Mexico. Catholic, naturally.

"The rebel government is in flight and we declare that all traitors will be executed and their land redistributed. The legitimate government of Mexico has already instituted emergency tribunals since last month to execute traitors and they say the tribunals are most busy.

"So you see Monsieur Bulloch, soon the Confederacy will have an ally on its side."

"And this Maximilian, he'll do what you say?" Bulloch asked. Gone were the formalities of before; matters had become too serious for indirect communication.

"Oui, oui, pas de problème. He is most, in English you say, supple. I repeat myself – supple. He will depend on us and he is not independent minded. I permit myself to say, he does not have much mind at all! He demanded we make public referendums, so we did, and one hundred percent of Mexicans were in accord he should be Emperor of Mexico! It's amazing! He never doubt the results! I think you Americans will find him a good neighbor."

Bulloch spoke after a moment of silence. "The price is substantially more than we had offered. The good people of the Confederacy offered a generous sum based upon the fair market value of the two ironclads."

"But Monsieur Bulloch, financial risk must carry a return. You are an intelligent man."

After hesitating pointedly, Bulloch said, "Well Lucien, we'll buy your ships. I'll sign."

He began to endorse the bottom signature line on the back page of the contract. "I do declare that, in the interest of our mutual friendship we'll consider the surcharges as gestures of Southern hospitality for our French allies. I reckon we will be able to count upon your steadfast support should it ever come to pass that we are in need."

Monsieur Arman just smiled serenely.

January 3, 1864

Juan Antonio drew his poncho closer to his body to stay warm. He and Garcia had drawn trail watch for the morning. They did not even have rifles or shoes, and the cold made them stamp their sandaled feet to avoid frostbite. It was winter, and in the mountains west of San Luis Potosí, there was snow on the ground.

The French had marched into San Luis Potosí just days before Christmas, forcing Presidente Juárez north to Saltillo. It was just a matter of time until they marched again.

South, in the capital, there was a "National Assembly" of thirty-five collaborators and former Conservatives, in addition to a ruling triumvirate. The government was essentially a puppet government with General Bazaine – who had fought under General Forey at Puebla the previous year and now had at his disposal over forty thousand French and collaborator soldiers – at the head.

Across the country, groups similar to the one Juan Antonio and Garcia had enlisted in since their flight from Puebla had coalesced.

Familiar with the local terrain and advised by the townspeople of enemy movements, the guerrillas lived like banditos in the hills, hiding by day and scavenging at night. There were several dozen members in this group, but a few more, filled with rage at the atrocities being committed by the French to terrorize the population, arrived every week. One man told of witnessing two men who were executed by burying them upright in the earth up to their shoulders and then stampeded over by horses. This ruthless cruelty only reinforced the nation's will to fight and nearly every young man Juan Antonio knew had vowed to resist until death.

"Hey, that's really something about your father isn't it?" Garcia interrupted Juan Antonio's daydreaming.

"Hmm?"

"You know, about how General Jeannigros lined up all the civil leaders in San Luis Potosí, including your father, at gun point. Then he asked them to sign the plebiscite 'imploring his Honorable Archduke Maximilian to come deliver Mexico from its plight'. The French never expected what we gave them back home. To think they believed we'd just surrender." Garcia gestured casually back to the east.

"Yeah, well, they still had to sign. And thank God they didn't suspect my father fought in the Army of the Center!"

"Our tenacity sure taught those gabachos something. They think we'll just roll over and play dead. Our neighbors went a day and a half without eating, locked up in jail together. If the old men can do that for the country, imagine what the young ones can do."

"Yes." Juan Antonio replied. "They don't understand that they'll never break our will. But first we need more volunteers and more weapons."

"We'll get them. Our ranks grow daily and the townspeople give us supplies. We can hide in the hills and attack when we're ready. I bet we don't even need to post lookouts; the villagers forewarn us whenever the French leave town."

"We still need to be cautious with their cavalry patrols." Juan Antonio looked wistfully at his red, numb feet. "Personally, I would rather have some boots and a rifle again before I start fighting."

"Whew. You're right about that. We wore those boots thin walking home from Puebla."

Juan Antonio thought back on the past six months: the long walk back north with other Puebla veterans, his father's return home and stories of Comonfort's cowardice and incompetence, the discussions on how to organize guerrilla groups, the vows to keep fighting... What they lacked in equipment they compensated for with courage.

The months with his family had been tense and poignant, the calm before the storm. From the day of his father's return, they knew it was only a matter of time before they were separated once again.

He removed his sombrero and ran his hand through his hair. It was getting a little warmer. Or was it his imagination?

"You know the norteamericanos still won't sell us arms?" he said to Garcia. "Presidente Juárez, our elected presidente of the Republic of México, keeps requesting them, and they still persist in only selling him a few old weapons and uniforms."

Garcia didn't avert his eyes from watching the trail in the valley below. "It's like Juárez says, wolves don't attack wolves. But we don't need the norteamericanos – the Cubans smuggled us arms! I read it in last month's *La Sombra de Zaragoza*. They also said that General Ortega escaped from French custody!"

"I heard the same thing. If it's true he probably returned to Zacatecas and we'll hear from him soon, maybe when spring comes and the real fighting starts up again. But you can't be positive with these newspapers. They write what they want you to believe. Here, I'll show you something." Juan Antonio threw back his poncho and dug into the folds of his clothing. From the interior of his pant's leg he produced a small piece of fabric, which he unwrapped. Inside was a neatly folded newspaper article.

"My father gave me this. He said he had never felt so betrayed in his life and he purchased two copies of the paper, one for him and one for me. It's from the tenth of June of last year but it didn't make it to San Luis Potosí until late autumn. It's a collaborator paper underwritten by the French. The good news is, if any soldiers go in our home, my father pretends he supports them! My copy I carry with me as a reminder of our struggle. This is from *La Soledad* – I'll read it to you."

"Today at eleven o'clock in the morning the French – Mexican army will make its solemn entry into the capital of México. After the army's triumphant entry, an event unparalleled in Mexican history, both in fact and the minds of the people, the people rejoiced in their political emancipation and newfound order and celebrated the end of eleven years of bloodthirsty conflict which had destroyed the country. The people saw in the banners of the army their salvation and hope. Those flags signify, as that of Iturbide, the return of order and union, lacking for so long in this nation. Liberators, welcome!"

Garcia was speechless for a moment, then he spat with vehemence on the ground before him and said emphatically "Traitors! They will hang for those words! That a Mexican could print such dishonorable filth!"

Juan Antonio folded the article in the cloth and put it back.

"Presidente Juárez said that after the war the editors of this paper and any other similar will be tried as traitors. Their time will come. Their time will come."

And they stared out at the mountain trail.

A CROWN FOR A FOOL

April 10, 1864

On the Adriatic shore, a husband and wife were in heated discussion. The couple was the archduke of Austria – Hungary, Maximilian and his wife, the Archduchess, Charlotte. They were talking in one of the many salons of the archduke's palace, close to the throne room, where envoys from Mexico waited to present him with the imperial crown and title of Emperor of Mexico and to receive his signature on the Miramar Convention.

The salon was opulently decorated; a massive Baccarat chandelier, with over a thousand crystals suspended from its gold plated arms, hung from the ceiling. Above the chandelier, the ceiling was patterned with gold leaves and the music balcony's rail was gilded. Over the fireplace hung a portrait of his brother Francis Joseph, emperor of the Austro – Hungarian Empire. Lacquered snuffboxes and porcelain bric-a-brac ornamented numerous pedestal tables around the room's perimeter.

"It just unsettles me, going out there while they're still fighting" Charlotte said. She was a fair woman of twenty-three with long, dark hair and a gaze that vacillated between careless joy and distraction.

"The fighting is nearly over." Maximilian replied. "They've taken most of the country now, and the rebel leader is now north of Monterrey, if not hiding in the United States. And the French did take a survey; six million, four hundred, forty-five thousand, five hundred sixty-four votes in my favor versus two million, one hundred seventy-five thousand, four hundred eighteen opposed. This one's for real! With such popular support we will certainly succeed."

"But France's support is not guaranteed... And I don't see how this offer is any different from the previous one that they made on the eve of the announcement of the London Convention. They didn't even inform you of that!"

"No, this time Louis-Napoléon committed in writing to support us. I personally demanded it when I went to Paris last month to discuss it. They will defeat the rebels and then leave a garrison of Legion Etrangère troops for another six years after the regular army departs. All they want in exchange is repayment of the entire war's costs up until its end, then one thousand francs plus transport costs per soldier extra, and repayment with interest for the French banks."

"But you have no guarantee, and those legionnaires are just criminals, outcasts on the run from their own countries."

"This time it is different. The war will only go on for a little while longer and this will be a boon for Mexico. I can implement all the reforms I was trying to achieve in Lombardo-Venetia. This is my one chance to be an emperor, not the mothballed younger brother of an emperor. We can build another Schönbrunn there. We'll import only the finest crystals and artwork, spare no expense! We will show the world how a liberated people can bask in the sunlight of an enlightened monarch!"

"Certainly it would be nice to be an empress again, and host balls," said Charlotte. "I mean balls that really matter. Ones that nobles cannot miss!"

"The Mexicans will love us." Maximilian said smoothly. "I wrote a letter to that Benito Juárez personally and proposed a truce. And the American government will warm up to us eventually; I'm positive of it! This vote of theirs, the unanimous resolution condemning a monarchy in Mexico will fade into obscurity. Now, I'm going to go accept the Imperial Crown that they brought all the way from Mexico in the throne room, and then we'll sail for Mexico on the *Novara* four days hence. This time is more serious than the last time the crown was presented. The world will soon see what a Hapsburg is capable of! Will you support me in this?"

"I understand this is our chance to regain true title and genuine prestige." Charlotte said. "I just want us to exercise caution. I fear we're being used. I think all your reasons to be reluctant in the beginning were correct."

"Perhaps. Yet once we're there I will assert myself and wrest control from Napoléon. He won't be able to dictate our actions all the way from Paris. We need this." Maximilian took her hand in his as he said this. It had been a long time since they had felt intimacy; unspoken humiliation had overpowered their affections as of late.

Charlotte looked at him. "Go. Accept the crown. We'll take our chances."

THE GRAND ARRIVAL

May 29, 1864

The port of Veracruz was as quiet as a graveyard at night. The huts along the waterfront appeared completely empty and nobody was walking in the streets. Only in the fort of San Juan de Ulúa, which defended the port, were there signs of activity. The Tricolore fluttered in the ocean breeze over the fort.

From the ship, Maximillian and Charlotte could see a small detachment of troops assembled on the dock. They had split into two ranks and it was clear that the he and Charlotte would walk between them from where the *Novara's* crew was formed, awaiting them.

The temperature and weather during the last few days had been insufferable. The breeze by no means compensated for the extreme humidity. Small wonder French casualties had been so high! *To fight in these conditions!* Maximillian thought. They would be certain to reside in a palace in the hills.

Maximilian stared out at the city of Veracruz. Normally the wharves would be bustling with commercial activity; sacks and barrels being loaded and unloaded, sails being stitched, men shouting and jostling one another. Aside from the soldiers waiting on the imperial entourage, he could not count more than half a dozen tan-skinned Mexicans. Well, with the stability of his reign, peace, order, and prosperity were not far off. After all, these pitiful subjects had known only strife and civil war since the Spanish left. Time for them to see the error of their ways.

After approximately ten minutes the launch was fully lashed to the wharf and they could step up onto the dock. As ceremony dictated, the Emperor was the first to set foot on his Mexico.

Maximilian climbed out with as much dignity as he could muster. A young Mexican man had come to his side and extended his forearm for the Emperor to lean on.

"Please be careful, Your Excellency," the young man said, attempting to speak German.

What an atrocious accent! They did not expect this fellow to be one of his servants, his German was awful! Should he switch to Spanish, lose face? How could he, speaker of seven languages, suffer the presence of so inept an assistant?

"Have nice trip?" the young man inquired, with an intent and eager expression.

What rudimentary understanding of the German language Maximillian thought. "Ja, danke. Sehr gut. We stopped at the Vatican en route. The Pope gave us his blessing to me to rule as a Catholic monarch."

Maximilian was safely on the dock now and his legs felt steady. He turned to assist Charlotte step out of the launch.

"There is a carriage for the Empress and me, right?" he asked the young man.

"Ja, Your Excellency. But General Bazaine wants that you know Veracruz before. It is before summer heat now, almost June, ja?"

"Since when does General Bazaine determine my itinerary?"

"Yes, Your Excellency. It's better to rest now, then see the capital. You are tired, true?"

Maximilian turned to Charlotte who nodded enthusiastically. They stepped away from the wharf to permit the crew to unload their belongings.

"Very well then. We'll stay in Veracruz. But where is the parade? Where are the celebrating people?"

"Yes?" replied the servant in an inquisitive manner as if he were responding to a question with a question.

"I said where are the celebrating people, the cheering crowd, the parade? Aren't they happy?"

"Yes, of course, Your Excellency. In Mexico City, Your Excellency." He bowed low as he said this and then turned to walk between the double file of soldiers toward a non-descript, open carriage with two horses harnessed at the front.

"What! That is our carriage! No imperial seal, no gilding? What kind of carriage is this?" The Emperor, very cranky from the voyage, was beginning to lose his temper.

"Yes, Your Excellency. It is just for go to fort. Not far, Your Excellency."

Charlotte sniffed in disgust at his side. Now he had her to placate as well!

They climbed into the carriage which did not even have extending footrests, just a bronze foot plate, and waited while their luggage was loaded.

"This is unacceptable." Charlotte said huffily. "You must complain to the French as soon as you can! There was not even a band!"

The carriage rolled toward the fort on the edge of the water. As it passed through the streets, the new rulers of Mexico saw dour faces staring at them from the street-level windows. Not one soul cheered or waved. In fact, if he didn't know better, Maximillian would have thought they were glaring at him! Perhaps it was the heat that made these folks so ill-humored. After all, they had voted for him!

INSPIRED BY THE CHALLENGE

June 1864

Emperor Maximilian placed his hands on the stone railing and gazed out over Mexico City. Up here one benefited from the breeze that broke the stifling summer heat and Maximilian enjoyed staring out over his country and pondering. About a month had passed since their arrival at Veracruz, and a few weeks since their arrival at Chapultepec Castle, which he had promptly renamed Miravelle in fond recollection of Miramar back home, as well as to break with any tradition that had Indian origin or reminded the Mexicans of any noncolonial period. Why, the Mexicans had even fought their last battle against the Americans' invasion from Veracruz less than twenty years ago in this place. Best to eliminate these links.

Looking out over the capital, beyond the walls manned by French soldiers, he mused on the daunting task that lay before him. Annually the Empire of Mexico spent 150 percent of what it took in, which was a paltry 12 million pesos. Almost three quarters of these expenses were for either foreign debt or military costs.

Rebellion was still active, principally in the north. The south was plagued by banditry and highwaymen. General Bazaine refused to renegotiate the terms of the French military assistance. However, volunteers from Austria and Belgium, as well as individuals from other central and eastern European nationalities, had started to immigrate here to fight on behalf of their emperor and empress. After the war these heroic patriots in the Legion Etrangère would be rewarded. It was they who had set the pace, shone forth as an example in places like Camerone, where sixty-five legionnaires had held back thousands of guerrillas who endangered the gold shipment for the soldiers besieging Puebla.

It was best to rely on Europeans; Mexican loyalty was questionable at best and if they were so smart, how had they let their country deteriorate into total anarchy? It was for this reason that he insisted every member of his cabinet be of European descent; Mexicans were too unreliable!

He shifted and strolled toward the garden. It was a beautiful garden, not so far set back from the balcony so you still perceived the elevation yet were concealed from the eyes of the city dwellers. He could feel at peace without incurring their envy and spite.

Anywhere else, the citizens could return his stare and he no longer deluded himself that he was liked.

Obviously the French had skewed their own survey.

Maximilian smelled the thick perfume of flowers as he entered the garden; multiple beds with paths in between circled a two story tower with statuette-filled alcoves on every first story wall, two per wall. The second story was circular, yet skirted by a square balcony built over the first story with triangular posts on the corners. The garden was flanked by a double-level walkway; the upper level was covered by the second story balcony terrace enclosed by stone railings and flowerpots. Unorthodox, but pretty in its own way. Botany was truly a science for the enlightened. Looking out over the railing, he stared out at the area where he had ordered a boulevard to be constructed to facilitate access from the castle to the city.

Inside, the Empress had set about redecorating almost immediately and orders had been dispatched to Sèvres and Limoges for the finest porcelain and crystal as well as Lucerne for clocks. Nothing civilized could be purchased on this continent, even American manufacturing had deteriorated with the destruction wreaked by their civil war.

But that American war could not go on indefinitely. Already the southern Confederacy showed symptoms of cracking. They must be sure to have amicable diplomatic relations with the Americans, because he was not fully sold on Napoléon's intrigues with the Southerners. Of course, they were preferable, but why alienate the Northerners?

Best to be accepted by everyone, be it the nations of the world or his own subjects. Already the Vatican, France, and England had recognized his government as the legitimate government of Mexico. Soon others would follow.

He stopped at the border of the garden then sat down on a bench.

A butterfly fluttered past his head. He gazed after it intently. He had not seen one of that species previously! There was so much on this continent to discover still.

His mind, inspired by the intellectual stimulation of one of his favorite pastimes began to race. He was naturally omitting a key ingredient to the success of his reign – the support of his subjects! With all this focus on European courts, he was overlooking their importance. They must never think that he did not value them or did not rule in their name, in their best interest!

Certainly, with his open mind the Mexicans would flourish under his benevolence! Charlotte was correct – the commoners must be appeased. She had already been to churches to distribute alms to the needy and he would adapt his behavior to accommodate the masses intermittently. Why he would even wear one of those huge shade-casting sombreros! Then they would cease calling him El

Austriaco. He would visit schools, hospitals, even prisons! He would become famous for his benevolence!

His mind accelerated still further with this new wave of inspiration. These people were so simple that occasional flourishes would sway their sympathies. Maximiliano, patron of the people! They could even evaluate an amnesty for former enemies of the Empire. Then the fighting would stop and they could have harmony. Everyone would live happily ever after!

He stood up and strode toward the entry hall which adjoined the garden. He must request a meeting with General Bazaine at once to get his approval. These were strokes of pure genius!

October 1864

The night was cloudy and there was only a quarter moon. This was preferable as the men would never be spotted as they crossed the high elevation points. They followed a man dressed entirely in black; instead of the usual sombrero he sported a black hat, black riding pants and a black shirt. As guerrillas they could ill afford to be noticed so they rested by day and moved by night.

Although they lived in the mountains like plateados, named for the silver they adorned themselves with from the loot of their victims, they could afford none of their extravagances. The men carried all of their permanent possessions with them as they maneuvered, either into villages to be given food or to attack French garrison troops.

It was like this throughout the country; everywhere the French controlled only as far as their rifles could reach.

This evening they were headed into the mountain town of Salinas, west of San Luis Potosí. It was a modest town but there were no French troops in it now, according to the townspeople and they needed to begin to stockpile provisions for the winter which was fast approaching.

There were almost forty men in their group but they communicated with other bands regularly. They had spent their summer ambushing French soldiers when they ventured in smaller units or moved between towns. The residents informed them of their movements and they reacted accordingly.

The guerrilla groups were still coalescing this year, but by next year they expected to be much larger and sufficiently organized to merge and attack in concerted campaigns. There was a rumor that they were relocating west to the Gulf of California to join up with Republican troops but their leader wouldn't confirm this.

The leader was an extremely stern man. He had actually fought against the Juárez government as a Christero, a Christian soldier fighting on behalf of the Catholic Church in the Guerra de la Reforma. At the end of the war he had been declared a traitor by the Church as he had refused to surrender and continued resisting. This had enraged him so much that now he had become a bandito in the hills.

Today, he fought in the name of Mexican independence. Juan Antonio believed it was just a convenient manner to live in the mountains and live through banditry. But whatever the reason, he was an adroit guerrilla leader, a ruthless warrior and he knew every footpath for miles. He taught the men to walk single file by night without illumination as well as how to step in one another's footprints to conceal their numbers.

At first, in only sandals, it was extremely difficult but with time Juan Antonio's eyes had grown accustomed to this.

Once, after ambushing a communications and transport convoy, they had taken a French prisoner. A message was sent into the town garrison on one of the captured horses requesting a ransom. No reply had been received, so after torturing the soldier by extracting his fingernails the man had been hung and left on the road between San Luis Potosí and Querétaro.

This was no different than how thousands of Mexican patriots had met their demise at the hands of the French, but Juan Antonio had to remind himself daily of that fact.

Ahead the group was starting to descend into an arroyo. They were drawing near to the town. Soon they would stop at the far end of the gully and disperse among the rocks to hide. From there several of them would make contact with the citizens and then, when all was clear, they would proceed.

The ground was rougher and rockier than the path they had just left and the rocks hurt Juan Antonio's feet through his sandals. He told himself it would hurt more if he had not lost so much weight in the past months living in the wild.

His thoughts drifted back to events in the north. Presidente Juárez still held the government together, although now he was in Chihuahua.

Further north, the norteamericanos seemed to be finishing their war. There was talk of a general marching through the south and the southerners were suffering defeat after defeat.

The column was halted and Juan Antonio walked to the side of the gully. He crouched behind a brush and hunched his shoulders up to keep warm. At least if they moved to the coast they would not have to march in the mountain snows!

He looked behind him at his closest comrade. He could just discern the outline of his body lying against the arroyo wall. There was no way to see in the darkness whether their eyes met and conversation was forbidden anyway.

A good amount of time passed and then Juan Antonio heard the muffled sounds of movement and the line began to snake forward crouched over. They were entering Salinas.

The arroyo led almost to the fence of a house; they had only to climb out, cross a stretch of twenty yards then walk through the fence that surrounded the house. The gnarled wood branches of a section of the fence had been removed and the guerrillas were crossing the yard, entering the house and returning again laden with sacks.

When it came to Juan Antonio's turn he crept out of the gully, scurried across the clear stretch and to the house. A little light radiated from lit candles in the interior.

As Juan Antonio entered the house followed by two of his comrades, he was surprised by what he saw – an elderly woman, wearing a shawl and a large silver cross around her neck, accompanied by an attractive young señorita, perhaps sixteen years of age. What was obviously their kitchen had been converted into a warehouse. The tables and chairs had been pushed against the wall and there were several dozen sacks of food in the center, apparently containing grain, rice, beans, and flour.

The men accepted the sacks handed to them by the two women and as the young girl handed Juan Antonio one she said with a quiet determination, "Viva México."

"Viva México!" Juan Antonio firmly replied as he slung the sack over his shoulder and disappeared into the night.

MIRAVELLE

December 1864

Emperor Maximilian regarded the Empress Charlotte from the opposite end of the table. She looked happier nowadays, content to be a genuine empress. She had her back to the fireplace which was bordered with carved wood. Above the mantle was a Biblical painting and on either side a bare-chested muse holding a lamp over her head.

These had been rough months. The rebellion continued, as did the popular discontent. The two of them hardly felt safe outside the grounds of Miravelle. In the towns outside the capital it was no different; the emperor's appointed representative was always subject to the local ranking officer's orders. He was forced to travel frequently, leaving Charlotte in charge of the ministerial meetings.

The emperor of France, Louis-Napoléon, had not kept his guarantees that Maximilian would be an emperor is his own right and he was obliged to consult with Marshal Bazaine before issuing any edicts. The Marshal himself did not face the same constraints and

Maximilian was constantly learning how Bazaine had superceded one of his directives before countless French and Mexican subjects. Bazaine had been promoted September 1st and now acted as the power behind the scenes in the Empire of Mexico.

Whatever the circumstances, they needed the French soldiers. The number of monarchist Mexicans that bore arms in his name was a scant seven thousand, and they were certainly not renowned for their reliability despite his initiatives to promote morale.

This had included knighting the Conservative generals Márquez and Miramón into the Legion of Honor. However, this had not been well received by the local population as they had become nefarious during the Guerra de la Reforma through their brutality and butchery.

Maximilian found himself dependent on an increasingly small quantity of loyal supporters. Still, he thought resignedly, those who stuck with him through the difficult times would be handsomely rewarded for their loyalty!

"How's the sausage?" his wife inquired, speaking in German.

"Schmeckt, danke." Speaking in German afforded them some privacy from their household servants.

"Did you see the photos from the American war? Just brutal, absolutely savage! It's an outrage that they let that photographer what's his name… Brady, just take photos of slain men in the field after battles. Those Americans are so uncivilized. Who wants to see such carnage in black and white anyway? I've never heard of it!"

Maximilian agreed. "Yes. I'll see to it that this new trend never reaches the Ere Nouvelle or La Razon but I can't control the foreign press."

"Well that man Matthew Brady ought to be hung! Civilized nations would never allow that! That's what democracy brings you. Photographing all the dead men and the mutilated horses. Ladies read the papers, see those photos. It's disgraceful!"

"Quite right," Maximilian concurred again "the worst part is that it is obvious that the American southerners will soon be defeated.

There is a Northern general called Sherman who is marching through Georgia as we speak, bisecting the South. The Americans have already begun diplomatic protests to us and the French about our regime. They assert that French soldiers in the Western Hemisphere are a direct violation of their so called Monroe Doctrine of 1823. Imagine! That's decades old!"

"And what shall we do about it?" inquired the Empress, putting her silverware down in a manner that implied pressure for him to act.

Maximilian sighed and rubbed his chin.

"For the time being nothing, my dear. We are the legitimate government of the Empire of Mexico. Already Austria-Hungary, Prussia, Spain, Italy, Belgium, and Portugal have recognized us. The United States will be forced to follow suit. Besides, I'm making diplomatic overtures toward them and they will be too weakened after their war to confront us."

A moment of silence followed. Maximilian wished he could guarantee the words he had just spoken.

He looked at the dining table and his surroundings. The Empress had done a splendid job decorating Miravelle to European tastes. Indeed, a small fortune had been spent on importing fine goods. Brocade curtains hung on either side of the glass paned doors to the balcony while a beautiful chandelier was suspended over the table. Its center light was adorned with a translucent semi-precious stone shade.

Sixteen chairs were placed around the table with seven on the sides. Each chair was bronze plated on the borders. Half a dozen candelabras in two rows of three were positioned on either side of a beautiful three level silver centerpiece filled with fruits and sweets. Their porcelain dinnerware bore the seal of the Empire of Mexico as did the base of every knife handle. Truly grand, but maybe a little ostentatious.

Never mind, with time all the Empire's debts would be settled, except the British. So much was owed to the British that even if the military costs of fighting the rebellion ended today they would still owe their shirts to the British!

Not that that softened Napoléon's persistent nagging for his money through his envoy here; the former finance minister of France, Langlais controlled Maximilian's books. Of course, at least this way he knew exactly where the money was going, even if he was unhappy about it.

One of the first acts of the new Cabinet, staffed exclusively by Europeans at his personal insistence, had been to place French accountants in charge of customs receipts at the ports and tax collection. They really had no choice in the matter – the French military could do what it pleased and it was the only way to appease their demands.

"How was the meeting with the Bishop?" Charlotte inquired with a raised voice projecting over the table.

"The usual. They want us to retract the Lerdo Laws and restore all their lands. They say they are short of funds and need compensation for supporting us."

"Well, they're not the only ones short of funds! Besides, with all the charity tours I do, distributing alms to their congregations they should not be so quick to ask for money. We can't please everyone you know."

"That's correct. Of course we need their support but they'll have to take a place in line behind Louis-Napoléon or Marshal Bazaine. They're who we have to make happy."

With that Maximilian picked up the delicate handbell to the right of his wine glass and rang it.

A Mexican servant entered and asked politely "Terminado?"

"Sí. Terminado."

LOS VERANOS

January 1865

Bang!

The Sharps carbine kicked into Juan Antonio's shoulder and the smell of gunpowder filled his nostrils. The French soldier threw up his arms and fell backward from the momentum of the projectile. Juan Antonio had been close enough to see his face as he trained his weapon on him. The French soldier was a sallow youth with sunken features and a pallid face. Now he lay on the road dead or dying in the province of Sinaloa.

Juan Antonio ducked behind the rock outcropping that served as cover for him and Garcia. The group of French soldiers against whom they were fighting were under General Castigny's command from the north of the town of Los Veranos.

He stuck his head over the rock again and carefully slid his carbine over the top. The winter sun shone brightly down on the western Mexican foothills around him.

Suddenly tiny rock chips hit his face. A bullet had struck the rock inches from his nose! Fortunately none of the fragments got in his eyes and after pausing to catch his breath and verify his face was undamaged he proceeded to take aim again.

The column of French soldiers had stopped and now they were all crouched down and firing to either side.

The guerrillas had begun the fight by firing upon the gabachos in the rear of the column. Then after the French had spun to face that direction, they opened fire in front of them, where Juan Antonio was, forcing them to shoot in both directions and blocking their movement either forward or backward. The guerrillas were badly outnumbered, but the French could not charge without completely exposing their backs and a withdrawal would expose them even more.

Bullets were ricocheting off the rocks in the earth near Juan Antonio's head. There were perhaps only thirty men on this side of the pass but they had put down almost as many French already.

He sighted his barrel methodically on a strangely attired man. The man was fair-skinned, so he was not a Mexican collaborator or a Zouave, yet he lacked the blue jacket and red cap of the French regulars. He wore a simple black low brimmed hat and a black vest over a white shirt and black pants. *Must be a Belgian mercenary or some other central European soldier of fortune* Juan Antonio thought.

Little matter, Juan Antonio squeezed the trigger and the man, hit in the face, was flung backward from his crouch and landed sprawled on his side, motionless.

Juan Antonio ducked back and Garcia asked, "Get the officer?"

"No." Juan Antonio responded and started to reload his gun. Casting a glance on either side he noticed one of his fellows had been hit. His comrades had dragged him back from the edge and his body had rolled down the slope.

"Here they come!" Garcia cried.

Other guerrillas were standing and firing down the slope. Juan Antonio peered over the edge and saw perhaps two dozen men, a large portion of the French side, running up the slope toward their position. They were not even pausing to aim their rifles and had not fixed their bayonets. Instead they were charging, holding their rifles before them perpendicular to their bodies to climb faster.

Juan Antonio scanned the line and spotted an officer. His cap had fallen off but his saber and jacket ornaments distinguished him.

He shouldered his carbine just as the officer cried out "Allez! Avancez!"

He fired at the officer's face, but the officer started forward just as Juan Antonio pulled the trigger and the round struck the ground behind him, sending up a cloud of dry dust. Cursed gabacho!

A wave of rage arose inside Juan Antonio and, witnessing his colleagues rising to defend the hill's crest and discharging their rifles, he shook his gun over his head, cried out, "El cinco de Mayo!" and charged directly at the oncoming French soldiers with an empty weapon.

There was only a short distance to cover between him and his opponent and he was running rapidly downhill toward the French. His eyes were fixed on the officer, and the officer leveled his saber at him, bracing for the charge. There were shots behind him and he believed his fellow warriors were following behind him but there was no time to stop and check.

A bullet whistled past his head but he was running so fast borne by so much momentum he would not offer an easy target.

He and the officer had locked eyes, and the Frenchman's stare was the only thing that Juan Antonio was conscious of. He could sense the officer's fear. In his peripheral vision Juan Antonio saw a French soldier fall backward, shot, and others began to wheel and run. But there was no more time to absorb anything else as he was practically on top of his target.

The man held his saber in front of him to stop Juan Antonio's charge, but Juan Antonio swung his carbine at it with both hands and knocked it aside.

Propelled by his forward momentum, Juan Antonio had only an instant to turn slightly as he ran full into the Frenchman, leading with his right shoulder. The collision flung them into the air, and for a second they tumbled down the hill together.

Juan Antonio landed on top of the officer and, although dazed by the impact, he heard the man grunt as he hit the ground with him on top.

Somehow Juan Antonio was still hanging onto his carbine. He staggered to his feet, his vision still a little blurry. The French officer was not holding his saber; it was a few feet farther down the slope. His jaw was slack and his eyes were glassy.

Juan Antonio, summoning all his strength gripped his carbine by the stock and swung it at the side of his enemy's head. The officer tried to parry the blow with his arm but it still landed. The weapon jarred his hands and the officer fell to the ground.

Switching his grip on the carbine to bludgeon downwards with the butt, Juan Antonio moved to stand over the officer. Still conscious, the man was holding his arms feebly in front of his face. Juan Antonio rammed downward with the butt, brushing aside the officer's arm and catching the man on the bridge of the nose. The man howled in pain and Juan Antonio raised the weapon again and drove it into his bloodied face. The officer's legs jumped up but his body went slack.

Juan Antonio's vision blurred and rage overtook his senses. A flood of memories swept through him; his father imprisoned and starved, countless nights sleeping and hiding in the mountains, villages razed and innocents executed, Mexican men in their prime hanging from trees on the sides of highways, fallen friends at Puebla.

A voice cried "Juan Antonio!" and someone grabbed his arms, preventing him from thrusting downward again. It was Garcia.

His head began to clear and the anger ebbed. He did not know how many times he had hit the man's face, but it was best not to look.

Glancing about, he saw the French were in full flight and his friends were shooting at them as they fled.

"They won't forget that anytime soon." Garcia said. "You killed the officer mano-a-mano."

Juan Antonio's heart was coursing with adrenaline. He couldn't catch his breath.

Garcia continued. "There were so many of them, but mercenaries are gutless and that's what half of them were."

Most of the guerrillas had come out from their ambush spots to take the weapons and boots from the slain enemy troops. Any wounded they left. The men were cold and had they despised their enemy any less they might have also taken their jackets.

Juan Antonio's head still spun with furor.

"General Corona is signaling for us to disband and meet again at the rally point" Garcia said. "We have to run now."

Juan Antonio followed Garcia at a trot. They ran back over the crest of the hill and through the surrounding scrubland, avoiding proximity to other guerrillas and minimizing disruption of the brush or deadwood, leaving as few traces as possible.

While they ran, Juan Antonio relived the moments of his headfirst charge down the hill. What had gone through the officer's mind as he saw Juan Antonio?

When they reached the rally point, they sat down and caught their breath. It took another ten minutes or so for everyone to make it back, minus the killed or wounded. After the count was taken, their leader, General Corona, spoke. "Muy bien. You all fought like diablos." He was walking around the circle of men with his hands clutched behind his back, pleased with his fighting devils.

"You," he said, indicating Juan Antonio. "One of the new Potosinos. I saw you lead the charge. If every man fought like you we would be fighting in France now, not México!" He patted Juan Antonio on the back.

"That attack will draw out General Castigny from Los Veranos. He will come north to try to punish us and rescue the wounded.

Last night, in keeping with our instructions, the townspeople of Los Veranos took all the French pack mules then abandoned the town. The town is empty now except for the gabachos. When the main force arrives north to locate us we will let them find us, or at least you fifteen over here."

He gestured to a portion of the men. "You hombres stay here and ambush them closer in. This is just to tie them down. The rest of us are going to retake Los Veranos. We have to move stealthily and be quicker than them, so take another fifteen minutes and then we'll move out."

When the group had started to talk a little, Garcia turned to Juan Antonio. "That's really something. We're starting to behave as a proper army again! One of the men was saying that there's similar fighting occurring in Michoacán and Guerrero. It's just a question of time you know; the norteamericano's civil war is almost over and they say that the gringos are demonstrating in front of the French embassy in Washington City! There are even norteamericanos volunteering to fight for us! Those gringos aren't so bad after all."

Juan Antonio flashed a smile back at him.

"Yes, last night one of the Sinaloans told me that in Lima, Peru, the countries of Peru, Chile, Ecuador, Bolivia, Columbia, Venezuela, and El Salvador all signed a treaty condemning the French occupation and demanding an end to it. Everyone knows if the French beat us they'll just move south. But then again, if the gabachos leave, we won't be able to kill them anymore."

"No. But like General Corona said, maybe we'll invade France? See how Napoléon likes it."

In a few minutes the men rose at the general's command and started to file after him, each man carefully stepping in their predecessor's footsteps and wearing their sandals backward to confound would-be trackers.

They marched like this for over an hour. When they neared Los Veranos, they were instructed to disperse laterally and lie silently in wait. Los Veranos was only perhaps half a mile away, visible below them.

The town was simple; only the church had a second story and this was merely a small bell tower. French troops were present, patrolling and tense, but few in numbers.

After some time spent in reconnaissance, Corona ordered half the men to come around the opposite side and in half an hour attack from that flank. Once they had launched their attack, the first group would attack also.

Half the group backed up, then circled around the pueblo while the remainder withdrew and waited. Although conversation was prohibited, Garcia glanced over at Juan Antonio and whispered, "This will be easy!"

Sure enough, after half an hour, loud shouts were heard, then gunshots. Their group rose to its feet and crossed the ground between them and the fringes of Los Veranos. They were almost to the edge when the French finally noticed them, distracted as they were. A few shots were fired at the charging guerrillas but this didn't slow them down. Juan Antonio found himself sweeping into the town as part of a mass of men, completely overwhelming the garrison.

The French were panic-stricken and overwhelmed; they fled first in one direction then the other to attempt to escape encirclement. Unfortunately a few did manage to slip through their closing noose.

Even after running through part of the town and checking abandoned houses Juan Antonio had not yet fired his gun.

A small group of French had locked themselves up in the church, and one of them began to ring the bell in the tower. He was felled within a minute, although it took maybe a dozen shots to hit him, because he was partially concealed by the bell tower walls. After he was hit, no one else dared to ring the bell even though they had locked the doors and the church was windowless. After a few moments of consideration, Corona gave the order to ignite the church doors.

While the majority of the guerrillas knelt in a semicircle facing the doors, sticks of wood were lit and placed next to the doors. To this was added discarded clothing from the homes and gunpowder from the dead soldiers. Lookouts were posted on the roofs of the houses and for half an hour the guerrillas watched the doors gradually burn.

When they were almost completely burned through the trapped soldiers struck them once with a pew, then on the second strike the pew flew through the remnants to land outside.

With a shout one, then two, then a third French soldier jumped through the doorway. They were met by a volley of bullets.

Juan Antonio had fired at the second solider. Such was the volume of balls fired that he could not even ascertain by their bodies' gyrations if either of the soldiers had been hit by his shot. The final soldier had not been hit quite as brutally as the first two and managed to remain standing after repeated bullet strikes, only crumbling to the ground lifelessly after clutching his torso and staring at the Mexicans.

The group was silent for a few moments, then Corona ordered; "Get their weapons and powder but take nothing else. Then ring the bell nonstop for fifteen minutes. Then we leave."

One of the men said almost admonishingly, "But, Señor. If we ring the bell the French will come."

"Exactly."

THE CONFEDERATE SAILING SHIP STONEWALL

January 25, 1865

It was evening and Commander Bulloch was waiting on the arrival of Captain Thomas Jefferson Page at his hotel in Vannes, France.

The winter on the Atlantic coast was rough, and this season the storms had been especially severe all along northern Europe. Vannes was tucked in a bay along the Gulf of Morbihan on the Brittany coast, and were it not for the occasion and the time of year, agent Bulloch would have found this to be an idyllic location.

The Bretons were a very traditional people, originally from the geographical area where Wales was now. Their language had Celtic origins. This made it even more of a challenge for Bulloch to get around but enhanced the secrecy of his passage. The Bretons lived as reclusive fishermen and boatmen, estranged from mainstream French society. They maintained their traditional garb and customs with the women wearing white bonnets.

South of Vannes, beyond the shelter of the bay, north of Belle-Isle, were anchored the CSS *City of Richmond* and *Sphinx* ironclad;

or should he refer to it as the *Staerkodder*? What a complex series of events had culminated in this surreptitious meeting in a small coastal town of Brittany.

Napoléon, sensing the Confederacy's weakness, had reneged on his offer to sell the four wooden corvettes and the two ironclads to them. The corvettes had been divided between the Peruvian and Prussians, and the Prussians, while still at war with Denmark, had also purchased the first ironclad, the *Cheops*. The second ironclad, the *Sphinx*, had been sold to the Danes, but because they had already been defeated by Prussia, losing a swath of their southern territory, they no longer required the ironclad.

It was trifle compensation that the French were offering reimbursement for the Confederacy's financial losses incurred by the cancellation of the sale. What the Confederacy needed was the ironclads, not promises!

Enter Captain Page and Monsieur Henri Arman de Rivière, intermediary agent and scoundrel with the influence to get the Danes to reject the ironclad, for a fee…

De Rivière was currently lodged incognito in a tiny hamlet called Arradon several miles outside of Vannes. Bulloch did not even believe there was an inn or a tavern for visitors there but it fit their need of secrecy very well. Captain Page was expected any time this evening on a rowboat at the Vannes dock.

Bulloch moved the frilly white cloth curtain over to the side of the hotel room's window to peer at the docks in the darkening light. The window looked directly out on the dock in this small coastal village. The entire square was paved with smooth, weathered stones. The architecture reminded him more of England than of France – tall, narrow, multi-storied buildings with straight, undecorated chimney stacks. The houses were built of grey stone walls and had bland, functional windows with wooden plank shutters. All this was reminiscent of the tastes on the opposite side of the Channel.

To his left, the square came to a point quickly at the main street and on his right the docks extended several hundred more yards.

Across the docks were the castle and fort, overlooking the small town. Any prying eyes curious about a large rowboat with two unidentified men inside would be in there. But, with the dark clouds it looked like it would be a stormy night.

Everything had been meticulously organized – de Rivière's unscrupulous forgery of the seaworthiness report declaring the vessel as nearly worthless to be rejected by the Danes, the smuggling of Captain Page to Copenhagen, the meeting for coaling and manning by a Confederate crew off the western coast of France. Even telegraph code phrases had been prearranged; Union spies were everywhere and their espionage reached even into French telegraph offices.

They were behind schedule, but it still appeared as if they would at last receive an ironclad. All for the modest sum of 375,000 francs for Monsieur Henri Arman de Rivière, a distant relative of the infamous Monsieur Lucien Arman who had built Bulloch's ships then sold them to different buyers, and 80,000 francs for a corrupt Danish banker named Puggard. Bulloch could not decide whom he detested more. If the Confederacy had had those ships last year, before the fall of Atlanta, or even at the end of '63, they might have turned the tide…

Bulloch heard footfalls in the square. Looking out the window again, he saw that the rowboat had indeed docked and two men were just climbing out onto the docks. They wore long cloaks with shoulder fringes and top hats but Bulloch knew instinctively they were Americans.

He rapped on the window as they approached the buildings, and when the men looked up, Bulloch waved until they saw his motions in the half-light. His lamp shone feebly and a drizzling rain had started – all the better to shroud their conference. He gestured for them to come up.

A few minutes later, there was a knock on the door. Bulloch opened it immediately. Before him stood a lone man.

"Captain Page, I presume."

"Yes sir, reporting as ordered."

"Come in, come in." Bulloch cast a glance down the hall to be sure nobody had seen Page enter, then he closed the door.

"Your associate?" he asked.

"He stayed downstairs to keep an eye out."

Page removed his top hat and cloak, a gentleman's disguise, to reveal the uniform of a naval officer of the Confederate States of America – steel grey jacket and pants lined with black silk serge, a double row of brass buttons down the front of his jacket, and double gold lace stripes on the cuffs. On his shoulders were epaulets and his collar had been pulled up to his chin. He was a partially bald man with curly hair who otherwise kept his beard trim and didn't sport a mustache.

"I do declare, Captain, you're well behind schedule. Trouble on the high seas?"

"You could say that, sir. Gales all the way, and the ship pitched like a seesaw. I reckon I've never seen anything like it myself." Page tapped the rain off his top hat and shook his cloak.

"So she's seaworthy?"

"Hardly, my dear sir. I don't know what you had to pay Monsieur de Rivière, but it was not a stretch of the imagination to have it declared unserviceable. Begging your pardon for my candor, but we did the Danes a favor!"

Bulloch exhaled through his lips in a sigh.

"Why I figure they knew this all along, they did." Page continued. "I don't believe this boat should be on the open water a't'all. It took us eighteen days to get here from Copenhagen. Outrageous! Have we paid these men?"

"No, my dear Captain, but we shall." Bulloch replied. "I'm of the same mind as you, but I have my orders. Richmond wants the boat under the name CSS *Stonewall* and, if you'll excuse the indulgence, beggars can't be choosers."

"With all due respect, how do you reckon I can sail that monstrosity... that worthless pile of scrap... to our cherished Dixieland?"

"We can arrange for you to make secret stops down the Iberian coastline. Hug Spain and Portugal then cut across to the Caribbean. I'll coordinate coaling tugs for you."

"Why, Commander Bulloch, it just pains my soul to see the French get away with this, after all we done helped them!"

"Well, no one wants to bet on a loser, Captain." A pang of regret at the bitterness of his remark passed through Bulloch and he looked away.

"Tomorrow morning I shall write Richmond." Bulloch said. "I shall also pay our contacts the monies for the *Stonewall*. Tomorrow night I want you to set your course for Spain. Write me when you're in port; we will render you all possible assistance. I will advise our allies there of your itinerary ahead of you."

Page nodded. "Devil of a scrape if I might say so sir. Disgusts me."

"Captain Page, what do you reckon you'll do after the war?"

"Sir?"

"You know – after the war. There's talk of men fixing to go down to Mexico or South America. They say Brazil's mighty fine and got lots of land for farming. What do you reckon you'll do?"

"Why sir, I plumb don't know. I imagine I'll just go back to the farm. Yes sir, I suppose I'll go back to my land." Page picked up his cloak and hat and walked to the door.

"Well, a good evening to you, Captain Page. Godspeed to you and your crew. Wire me from Spain; keep me abreast of your progress."

After Captain Page had departed Bulloch watched him out the window. The drizzle continued unabated and a mist had rolled in. Page and his crewmate boarded their rowboat and rowed out to sea.

Long after they were lost from sight Bulloch continued to stare out the window at the dark, roiling Atlantic.

May 22, 1865

Juan Antonio and Garcia were in the city of Chihuahua in northern México. Their men had been repositioned to the north to help defend the seat of Presidente Juárez's government, for the time being installed in Chihuahua, a city famous for its beautiful cathedral with its ornate façade.

To the west were the Sierra Madres, which provided shelter for the Republican soldiers, and surrounding the city was the Chihuahuan desert which permitted easy tracking of French maneuvers in the region as they pushed northwards.

Many events had transpired in the months since their battles in Sinaloa. A new Army of the Center had re-formed as a formal fighting unit in Michoacán, and the number of Republican volunteers increased daily, while the desertions among the French forces mounted due to demoralization and loss of confidence. The Belgians especially earned a reputation for looting and brutality, while the Zouaves began to actively rebel against being forced to fight in México. There had even been Zouave defections to their cause!

In the north, the American president Abraham Lincoln had succeeded in abolishing slavery in the southern United States, and the supreme commander in chief of the Confederate forces, Robert E. Lee, had surrendered and the rest of the Confederacy had followed suit. Shortly afterward Abraham Lincoln had been assassinated. Even in México, the news had spread like wildfire.

Approximately two weeks ago, Presidente Juárez had received the first shipment of American arms from a Union convoy. Finally the norteamericanos had selected a side! After years of buying nonessential supplies the government of the Republic of México could finally purchase weapons of first-grade quality. The Monroe Doctrine had become more than ideology.

That day Juan Antonio and Garcia were to help oversee the transfer of the purchased weapons from an American convoy to their possession on the outskirts of town and were marching there now with a group of men.

The Chihuahuan terrain was mostly flat, although there were some foothills. By and large the earth had a burnt look to it, and there was sparse vegetation. The earth was very rocky and broken. There was a chaparral corral where they were to meet the wagon train, escorted down from the border, for the transfer. There were some new weapons inside that the men were to be trained how to operate.

Following the men were three carts on wagon wheels, drawn by burros. The temperatures were still not too hot and there was a breeze, so their assignment was not intolerable.

When the group arrived the two American wagons were already there.

The wagons were of typical norteamericano build; a large wooden plank bed on four wagon wheels with a driver's box that could fit two men seated on a small bench. Each was covered by a large white canvas top supported by wooden ribs to make a white tent back.

The norteamericanos were waiting for them to arrive. There were six of them: two drivers, three soldiers, and an officer.

This was Juan Antonio's first time to ever lay eyes on a norteamericano, or gringo. Their skin was as pale as the gabachos, and all but one of the drivers sported a mustache and or a beard, or both. The drivers wore wide-brimmed hats, plaid shirts, and pants held up by suspenders. All of the soldiers had blue uniforms, blue caps with the emblem of a bugle on top, and a black leather strap to tighten or loosen their fit, and a single row of brass buttons on their blue jackets, which had upturned stiff collars.

Two of the soldiers had stripes sewn on their arms, an insignia of rank. Their boots were black leather with laces but their pants were grey. Their knapsacks were slung diagonally over their backs with a leather belt festooned by a silver buckle. One of the soldiers even wore spectacles.

The officer looked resplendent in his uniform. Here was the epitome of a fighting man. His larger blue hat had the initials "*U.S.*" stitched into the front and fringed with gold braid. Under his jacket, he wore a white shirt and on his shoulders were sewn rectangular gold braids. He also wore a sword and white kid gloves. He had come on his own horse, which he held by the reins beside him now. It also was branded with the initials "*U.S.*" and had saddle bags slung over the rump.

Their group approached and stopped, backing the carts up to within a few yards of the wagons. The norteamericanos cast glances at one another and shifted on their feet anxiously. The officer lifted his hat off his head ceremoniously then said something in English to their translator.

The translator responded to him and then, turning to Juan Antonio's group, said, "He's going to show us the rifles, then we load them on the carts."

The American officer issued an order to the three soldiers and the two drivers, and they climbed the wagons and began to pass out small crates and place them on the ground in front of the wagons.

The officer was bent over one of the crates which were unmarked. He used one of the soldier's bayonets to pry off the planks, and when he had removed the top planks he reached under the straw and pulled out a short, stubby rifle the likes of which Juan Antonio had never seen before. The barrel was maybe the length of a man's arm, and where the trigger was, there was some sort of lever attached.

The American officer spoke again to the soldiers and they produced an empty crate and a small bag stamped "*U.S.*". The officer continued to unpack the unique rifles until eight were leaning against the crate.

"They will demonstrate the new repeating rifle." the translator explained. "Less than half a year ago Presidente Juárez dispatched General Ortega to the United States to negotiate the purchase of the latest in weaponry – repeating rifles."

Juan Antonio and Garcia exchanged glances. So that was what had become of General Ortega! Well, he had indeed delivered!

The officer was loading small bullets into the metal part near the trigger – not the mouth of the barrel! He also was loading many bullets one after the other! What was this new rifle capable of?

The soldiers had set the empty crate on its side about a hundred yards away from the officer, placed the sack on top, and then returned to the wagons.

The American officer turned to address them and began to speak to them in English. They had to wait for him to finish and the translator to tell them what he had said.

"These are the new Henry repeating rifles. They can hold sixteen rounds, and in the hands of a trained shooter you can kill as many men in fifteen seconds. The lever reloads. He will now demonstrate."

When the translator was finished, he nodded to the officer who lay down behind the recently unloaded crate with his rifle, resting the Henry rifle on the top. The man pushed back his hat, squinted, and then emptied the rifle in what seemed to them like a drum roll. Several in the Mexican group let out gasps. The sack, which had been placed as a target on the empty crate, had been hit multiple times and lay in tatters behind it.

The officer stood and said something to the translator. When he had finished, the translator spoke.

"He said that we have two hundred and forty of these rifles, as well as ammunition and Colt revolvers. Our government has purchased them. There will be more shipments, and most likely, even volunteers, when the south of their country is fully secured. These rifles change the way men fight. Defensively, small groups can hold positions against much larger units and ambushes will be more effective. He wants us to help them unload the rest of the crates and put them on our carts."

Their group started to help the norteamericanos carry the crates over to their burro wagons. The atmosphere was light and jovial; the two groups flashed smiles at one another, nodded their heads, and patted one another's arms. They exchanged hellos and holas.

Juan Antonio's mind was racing. With weapons like these and their numerical superiority there was no way the French could win!

When the transfer was complete, the American officer saluted their group, mounted his horse, lifted his hat in one hand and with the reins of his steed in the other he said, "Vaya con Dios."

With that he turned and the norteamericanos began to return north.

The Mexicans prodded the burros and headed back to town, confident of imminent victory.

THE STARS AND BARS

June 26, 1865

The Confederate cavalrymen looked out across the Río Grande to the Empire of Mexico. At the head of the group was Brigadier General Joseph Orville Shelby, commander of the Fourth Missouri Cavalry, more commonly known as the Iron Brigade.

Resplendent in Confederate grey adorned with flowing golden braiding tracing his arms and collars and sporting a short black beard with flowing black hair under his hat, he led a group of one thousand volunteers – rebels who had refused to capitulate to Yankee rule.

They represented some of the most gallant men ever to bear the Stars and Bars in arms. Each of them, upon learning of the capture and subsequent surrender of President Jefferson Davis, had mustered to Shelby's call for continued resistance from Mexico. He proposed leading them south where the Confederacy would rise again like the phoenix from the ashes. Secesh would live!

The men had marched across Texas through Austin and San Antonio to Eagle Pass. Along the way they had armed themselves with French and English weapons, abandoned in munitions depots after having been imported via Matamoras, Mexico, in exchange for Southern cotton. They now possessed a full battery of ten horse-drawn Napoléon cannons, as well as six thousand English Enfield rifles and four Colt revolvers for every man, in addition to his Sharps carbine.

In passing through Texas, they had fought to re-impose order on the remnants of the imploded Confederacy, defending the towns and cities from the depravations of looters and pillagers. They had even held the Austin subtreasury safe from robbers. Followed loosely – or rather escorted out – by Union soldiers, they had been an island of order in an ocean of lawlessness.

On the opposite side of the Río Grande, or Río Bravo del Norte, lay Piedras Negras. It was held by Juaristas loyal to the Mexican Republicans in flight. Beyond them – desert.

By hook or by crook, they would get access to a Pacific seaport that could serve as a rallying point for the Confederates in flight. Already hundreds had crossed into Mexico and, with a new capital, by Jove, they would retake the South!

But who would they deal with? Benito Juárez – or Ferdinand Maximilian and Achille Bazaine?

Shelby moved his steed into the waters of the river and, with a gesture, Colonels Elliott, Williams, Gordon, Slayback, and Blackwell carried the Iron Brigade's tattered Stars and Bars into the Río Grande, splashing as they went.

To bear these colors into Mexico would be an act of overt aggression. Already they faced two potential enemies and had not yet made an ally.

Shelby lifted his hat and the men placed a rock on the flag. It sank into the murky waters, never to fall into Northern hands.

The South is dead! Long live the South! Exile over surrender!

And the Iron Brigade followed Shelby across the Río Grande and into the territory of the Empire of Mexico.

UNDER PRESSURE

July 1865

Emperor Maximilian walked quickly down the hall. On the left, in the salon, sat Charlotte, idly playing cards with a maid.

How could she so casually distance herself when the situation was so bad? The more the army fought, the more the rebels' ranks swelled. It was like trying to slay a hydra! No, she had the easy role: to travel to sites giving out alms and playing benevolent Empress. Not long ago she had gone to Zitacuaro, fifty miles to the west, to restore the public image damage caused by Belgian legionnaires who had razed and looted the town. As right she should have – it was her people who had rampaged, digging them an even deeper hole than they were in now!

He reached the end of the corridor and stepped out onto the balcony to look over the city. Below, the calm of the capital belied the reality of the situation. How could he repay the foreign debt to the British and the French when the war alone now consumed twice the government's annual revenue?

Maximilian knew that without the highly paid elite guards and their cannons protecting the castle, it too would be under siege. And now how would the Mexicans respond to the news that their taxes, raised severely last year, would now be doubled again? If they would just cease fighting, he could restore order to the country. Didn't they realize what an enlightened monarch he was?

The summer heat did nothing to alleviate his stressed nerves. On the contrary, it merely exasperated him further. He reentered the hallway. One of the servants was there, dusting the wooden table underneath the blue and white porcelain vase imported from Canton, China. The servant stopped what he was doing and bowed respectfully.

Well, at least one of the natives knew he was the Emperor! But Emperor of what? Perhaps it was time to return to Austria-Hungary? He had renounced all claims to the Austro-Hungarian throne, but maybe his older brother would show leniency. His correspondence from his mother indicated otherwise, but maybe they could still get back. Surely the Hapsburgs would not abandon one of their own? Besides, there were tidings of war in Europe.

That cursed Prussian prime minister, Otto von Bismarck, spoke of a German Confederation excluding Austria but incorporating the northern states under their control. Well if it was war they wanted, then the Austro-Hungarian Empire would let them have it!

The Emperor entered his office. There on his wooden writing desk lay another document. He walked over to read it.

Another formal protest by the Americans! They had grown more vocal since the end of their civil war. Of course, the defeat of the southern Confederacy had precipitated an influx of Confederate volunteers, who had been integrated into the Foreign Legion with the Arabs and Europeans. But that new president in Washington, Andrew Johnson, could not be put off. Just in May they had sent a general to the border to initiate troop movements in a vain attempt to intimidate him. The indignation!

Yet, one needed to be careful with them.

With a sigh, he seated himself to write a reply to the Americans. What more non-committal nonsense could he write this time? He had enough problems to contend with without the Americans trying to behave like world dominant Europeans.

July 1865

General Shelby walked toward the entrance of the dining hall where a banquet in the brigade's honor was about to be held. He was accompanied by several of his top officers.

They had marched almost two hundred miles from the Río Bravo del Norte to Monterrey and so much had transpired in the interim: a declined offer from the Mexican Republicans to join forces and the subsequent sale of their artillery and much of the surplus small arms on the premise that, upon their departure from Piedras Negras, they would be considered enemies of the Republic of Mexico.

This promise had been upheld; as from that day forth the column had been beset by guerrillas during every storm, or at night in their bedrolls, or at river crossings. The scoundrels were so ill-trained they always suffered grievous casualties while the Iron Brigade's own losses had been light. Nevertheless, the Mexicans were a force to be reckoned with.

Add to this a fierce battle at a river ford with a mixed force of Mexican desperados and Lipan Apaches, who killed irrespective of nationality - and you could understand why the men were happy to have arrived at Monterrey.

Five thousand French soldiers, legionnaires and Zouaves, held Monterrey under the command of General Pierre Jean Joseph Jeannigros.

Shelby and his men were bivouacked in the city at the general's order under a flag of truce and soon Shelby would break bread with him. Time to determine where the French allegiances lay!

The city was flush with recently arrived Confederates on the run and it was from them that Shelby had learned that Jeannigros already knew of their sale of arms to the Piedras Negras guerrillas. There would be some explaining to do, but nothing he in thirty-four years hadn't faced in the past. So long as they wouldn't be drinking any of the French fire water, absinthe, that the French soldiers were wont to drink, he would keep his cool.

Shelby and his subordinates entered the room dressed in their best grays and with their boots freshly polished.

In the center of the room was a long table set with silverware and porcelain, as well as with pewter candleholders. The table was filled with French officers and some Confederates, and all rose to greet them. A plump, bushy-bearded man perhaps fifty years of age at the head of the table tapped a knife against his wineglass and said in English "Enter cavalrymen. We welcome you!" *General Jeannigros.*

With a toast to the arrival of the Iron Brigade, the men, Confederate and French alike, seated themselves. Everyone poured wine into his own glass because the bottles had been opened previously in keeping with the French custom of letting the wine breathe prior to consumption. Servants began delivering food as soon as Shelby and his men sat at the table. Conversations began.

Jeannigros spoke fluent English and, after his first glass of wine, he looked straight at Shelby and asked "So, my good soldier, what news from the north?"

Shelby placed his glass on the table and replied. "Much news unfortunately. We were ambushed by rebels almost the entire trip. Ne'er a ford was crossed without some sort of skirmish and the cowardly curs always attacked at night. Yet, I reckon for every good American soul that lies quiet now there must be ten banditos who'll ne'er trouble us again."

"Impressive, General. Most impressive. But it would be easier next time if you don't sell them your weapons to kill you with, non?"

"Right indeed, my dear sir. That was a most complicated manner. I reckoned it wiser to sell them what we had to abandon, as in any case we could not be burdened like a regular army unit. Why, we done received sixteen thousand dollars for them munitions. For men who seek an alliance with your side, I figure you oughta view it as a fair trade."

"That is not for me to judge. As we French say, you must always look to the right and the left. As for alliance, you must talk with Le Marechal. But here in Monterrey you are my invités. Bienvenue chez nous!

"I propose a toast to our American allies who have come to support us!"

With that, Jeannigros stood and raised his glass to Shelby. Everyone at the table followed suit and new drafts were poured. Shelby remained standing after the toast.

"General Jeannigros, pray tell of the men at Camerone. They were under your command were they not?"

With an acquiescent flip of his left hand and a nod the general spoke.

"Camerone... Camerone." Shelby sat down and Jeannigros straightened his stunted beard between his thumb and his forefinger.

"Camerone. Colonel Dupin, shall I tell them of the glory of our legionnaires?"

Everybody looked toward the center of the table. There sat a tall, gaunt man over sixty who looked as if he could kill a man with a look.

His hair was as white as snow and his eyes even colder. Earlier he had introduced himself as Colonel Francois Achille Dupin, Contre Guerrilla.

"Pourquoi pas, mon General." Dupin's voice was as grave as an executioner's.

"Well then. I commence." Jennigros said. "But I tell you in such a way that you fully understand the honneur, the courage, the sacrifice that these men made for the glory of the Legion."

He emptied his wineglass, refilled it, then drained it again.

"My friends. I have had the privilege to serve in the French military for three decades. I have been wounded thirteen times, fought with the Emperor to depose the Second Republic in the coup d'état of '51 and have campaigned in Europe, Africa, Asia, and now the Americas. I saw the artillery duels at Sebastopol, where it seemed as if the very wind were composed of cannon shot. I saw the Light Brigade charge there and the Czar surrender. I witnessed carnage on the fields in Italy at Solferino so horrific that it seemed man was but a lemming intent on racing to his own death. That Swiss man, Jean-Henri Dunant, founded the Red Cross after having seen the same things I saw with these eyes.

"I have fought black-robed Chinamen with oriental swords and pikes. I have gone sabre to scimitar against Arab riders who seemed to materialize out of the shimmering desert heat as if part of a mirage. Yet before the sacrifice at Camerone I am a humble man.

"Towards the end of the siege of Puebla, when the rebels had almost starved I received orders in Chiquihuite, inland from Veracruz on the road to Puebla, to protect an inbound convoy carrying artillery and over three million in gold for General Forey, that peacock who took Mexico City without a fight and paraded for hours in his own honor.

"My third regiment under Captain Jean Danjou, a veteran who had lost his right hand in the Crimea when his rifle exploded and used a wooden replacement, was depleted to sixty two men and his two second lieutenants. Nevertheless, they volunteered to be the vanguard for the precious convoy, fully cognizant of the guerrillas active near our supply lines.

"They left our encampment under the cover of darkness on thirtieth of April, 1863 at one in the morning. Shortly after sunrise they realized they had been trailed by Mexican cavalry who subsequently charged them.

"The men withdrew to the ruined village of Camerone. There they holed up in a destroyed hacienda which was overgrown by vegetation on three sides, providing obstruction against cavalry charges. They were encircled by over two thousand guerrillas as the cavalry were soon joined by foot infantry, all of whom smelled the scent of blood.

"Multiple offers of parley were extended and declined, and the sixty five men were charged repeatedly, sustaining heavy losses yet never being overcome. By six in the evening the Mexican commander ordered an all out assault to finish them off before nightfall. By then, the legionnaires fired from behind barricades of human corpses. Still they held, and when they were down to twelve, all wounded, only five could move and only five cartridges remained, were they captured."

Jeannigros refilled his wineglass, drank the contents, and cast a glance at his audience. Everyone listened with rapt attention and some of the French officers had bowed their heads.

"This we know from a certain legionnaire named Lai who, stabbed seven times and shot twice, had been taken for dead by the Mexican dogs. So base were these guerrillas that they left all the bodies of the slain stacked in a pile when they left the battle site. Left for dead inside the pile of corpses and certainly near to it himself, Lai waited until nightfall then climbed out from under the bodies to try to regain Chiquihuite.

"When the news reached us of the fight I went there personally with some grenadiers. At daybreak on the second day after the fight on the road to Chiquihuite we found Lai half naked and on the brink of death. He could barely communicate what had happened but we learned nevertheless. He lives today, by the way, recipient of our Medaille d'Honneur.

"It is at times like these that one looks to men like Colonel Dupin." He gestured to the cruel looking old man who did not speak English and had been taciturn until now.

"Dupin is a natural hunter. War is his home, his mistress, his reason for living. Expelled from the army after the China campaign for brutality, and relieved of his countless medals, we invited him here to Mexico as a legionnaire for, as you know, the Legion Etrangère turns its back on no man. And we need killers like Dupin; they're good at what they do. We are fighters, not politicians, and we leave the moralizing of the methods up to them. They need us to fight; we do it. What importance then are a few rapes, a few murders, in a land of utter lawlessness? But I digress.

"Dupin gathered a posse and set out after those dogs. He ran them down for seven weeks through the hills. They could not run fast enough! I will spare you the boring details but rest assured, Camerone was avenged!"

Jeannigros thumped his fist on the table and Dupin stared fixedly forward, devoid of emotion.

"Qu'est ce que tu penses Dupin?" Jeannigros asked Dupin what he was thinking.

"Je dis toujours, mon General; tuer est sacré." Killing is sacred. The room was dead silent.

"So, when Marshal Bazaine, who was a lowly general back then – as I was a lowly Colonel then, too – replaced General Forey I petitioned for the name of Camerone and the date, 1863, to be written on every Legion Etrangère flag. And so it stands today."

Jeannigros poured wine into his glass and raised it.

"Gentlemen, I propose a toast."

Everyone stood.

"To the legion; Honneur et Fidelite!"

Everyone lifted their glasses and took a drink.

"To Camerone and the bravery of the legionnaires who saved the convoy. To Captain Danjou of the wooden hand!"

They drank again.

"And to Colonel Dupin, our killer and their avenger."

They emptied their glasses.

The men sat again and conversation resumed. Jeannigros related stories of martial glory and the Tricolore, while both sides discussed the impact of the Confederacy's surrender would have on the America. It was a friendly reception, yet inconclusive. They would need to go to the top and the top was in Mexico City.

CHANGE IN THE AIR

July 1865

The carriage rode through the streets of Noyon without stopping. Emperor Louis-Napoléon III could not resist peeking outside the coach at the twin towers of the magnificent cathedral. The matching triangular topped towers stood like sentinels over this part of the Oise region. They were visible on the left over the livery and stables.

Out the opposite side of the carriage they were passing by the Hôtel de Ville. It was an ornately decorated structure with eight windows on the second-story façade, flanked by bordered alcoves. A sentry stood by the double wooden doors out front and he stared at the moving coach.

The Emperor pulled his head back from the glass and pushed the red curtain across the window. Secrecy was of the utmost importance here. His movements must not be known.

It was for this reason that he traveled in a lone carriage without a coat of arms and with only the two coachmen, who were armed with concealed pistols. Other horsemen proceeded and trailed his coach to dissuade highwaymen, but far enough away to not be linked to the plain black carriage that raced out of Noyon to the north. He himself was armed with a brace of pistols, loaded, and charged, laid out in the case on the pillows next to him.

Prussia, Prussia, Prussia! There was no denying its territorial ambitions now.

There was talk of a German confederation controlled not from Vienna but from Berlin! Now Prussia and Austria had taken Schleswig from the Danes. Otto von Bismarck played for time – promised to consult him on any strategic move that the Prussians made. They were rising fast.

But, the men of Brandenburg would not redraw the map of Europe so easily! Not with all their seven-foot tall, goose-stepping soldiers could they beat the Second Empire. Yet, the best French troops were committed in Mexico, or honored the soil in that land with their graves, killed by yellow fever or rebels' murderous bullets.

What a fiasco Mexico had become! Installing a man such as that sniveling Maximilian had proven to be a double-edged sword; incompetent enough to manipulate but simultaneously too incompetent to rule! Already France's window of opportunity to forever stunt the American expansion had closed irrevocably. They would give him a few more months – half a year at the most – then tough decisions would need to be made.

And no coming back home for him – even his own family wouldn't have him back. Besides, that was the last thing he needed was that whiner moping around the courts of Europe sobbing about how he was wronged and misunderstood!

But what to do with the man who had become such a liability? Leave him to die? Tarnish French honor?

They were out of Noyon now so it was safe to look outside again. The Oise was such a picturesque region; rolling green hills, rich in trees and brooks and replete with fertile soil. The road was hillier now and the carriage rolled up and down sequential hills. They were making good time now and would reach the rendezvous with the Hanoverian military attachés by evening.

Ever since the Confederation of the Rhine the Hanoverians had affiliated themselves more with England or France than with the Germans, and now, before the rising Prussian menace to their independence, they sought the Empire's assistance. He felt it ironic that it was his uncle that had delivered Hanover to the Prussians and now they dealt with the French to secure their position.

Now, together with the Austrians, would be the most opportune time to squelch these upstarts. But, with the crème de la crème of the armée across the Atlantic, the Empire could ill afford a second war. That was the mistake his uncle had made. And the withdrawal of troops protecting the Pope in Rome from Italian nationalists who demanded Rome as a capital was still not finished. What would happen to the Holy City after his soldiers, checking Italian annexation under Garibaldi, left? None of his projects were working out.

The carriage passed alongside a farmer walking in the road. He looked up straight at the Emperor's face but did not give any overt signs of recognition. Well, with his top hat pulled low and his handlebars twisted and waxed to be especially thin, there was no reason to believe he was the Emperor. Nevertheless, he closed the curtain again and leaned his head against the wood paneling of the back wall of the coach. Prussia was a higher priority than Mexico; Maximilian would have to be cut loose.

A strong breeze swept over the hills of the Oise and shook the carriage.

August 5, 1865

Presidente Juárez stepped out of the stagecoach to stretch his legs. The rear wheels of this coach were enormous, so it had been a stable journey up to this point.

The heat of the Chihuahuan desert between the Chihuahua and the Río Bravo was stifling even to sit in. He began to walk into the desert; a little fresh air would revive him from the monotony and lethargy of the road. There were cactuses growing in this part, a clear indication that they could not be far from El Paseo del Norte on the Texas border. Their forces controlled most of the towns on the Río Bravo and they needed to withdraw there.

He sighed. Once again he had been displaced to another city.

He had really appreciated the beauty of Chihuahua – the cathedral, the citizens, his home four blocks from the Plaza de Armas. But, as the saying went, it was always darkest before the dawn. They would retake the city next year, when the French offensive had fizzled. They needed to be patient only a little while longer.

He glanced back at the stagecoach convoy. He must not stray too far from them. His guards were observing him discreetly, making sure he did not get bitten by a rattlesnake or attacked.

Victory was certain; already his generals conspired to position themselves in the post-French México. Even Jesús González Ortega plotted against him from the safety of the United States, and south of Chihuahua they formed alliances to share power undemocratically. Word of French overtures to his generals had reached his ears from other members of Congreso. Certainly none of them could be so foolish as to switch over. Besides, the Congreso was sure to extend his authority again. The unity behind him was irrefutable.

He halted and stared at the brown earth before him. *Nuestra tierra – our land.*

How could the thirst for power warp a man's vision of this simple truth? The thirst to rule over other men was so seductive; in all his years, he had known only betrayals by even his closest associates once they rose to the top. Could he himself say with a clear conscience at heaven's gate that he had always resisted temptation? His childhood had been so difficult, the death of his Zapactecan Indian parents shortly after he learned to speak, his childhood with his uncle until the age of twelve, his years of toil and self instruction in Oaxaca. Why had Dios burdened him so?

"Señor Presidente, we should be leaving now." One of his attendants had come to where he was standing.

He waved his acknowledgement and headed back to the coach.

He must face life's challenges one day at a time.

THE EMPEROR AND THE RULER

September 3, 1865

Marshal Bazaine walked into the office of Emperor Maximilian. He was over fifty and white-haired with a receding hairline, yet sported a black moustache and goatee. Although he was pudgy, the corpulence belied his complete power. He was the most influential man in Mexico.

The Emperor looked up and beckoned him to sit before his desk.

Over twenty years his senior, the Marshal had never previously collaborated with an individual whom he considered so naïve and befuddled. Of course, this made Maximillian all the more malleable.

"Bonjour, Maréchal. Asseyez-vous."

Good. The Marshal preferred to converse in French. He took a seat as invited by Maximilian.

"So, this morning the Americans arrived. They are about eight hundred strong and have already requested an audience with you."

"Anything new?"

"No, Your Excellency."

"Well, as we discussed they represent a double-edged sword. Gallant and loyal fighters, undoubtedly. But far too few in numbers to ever remotely halt the tide of American soldiers that would come to eliminate them if we accept their assistance. The Americans have over one million battle hardened veterans in arms and mustered, fresh from the crucible of war. To bring this down upon us would be pure folly."

"I think they're good soldiers, and if they'll serve in the Legion Etrangère we can use them."

"Yes, but they won't. They bring their own agenda. The fact that they tried to make for the Pacific until we ordered them here establishes this. They are such excellent fighters that I fear we would not be able to control their actions."

"Emperor, they lifted the siege at Matehuala and saved Major Pierron and the Eighty Second Infantry from annihilation. They charged into the Mexican picket lines and scattered the guerrillas with a six-shooter horse charge that swept them away like leaves in the wind. We need men like that."

"Yes, but that's what frightens me." Maximilian replied. "They are unquestionably good men, as are all the Confederates who have come to the capital or the rest of the Empire. Yet to enlist them is to invite the wrath of the United States. I believe we can reach a diplomatic compromise with our northern neighbors and to accept these men in a military capacity would be akin to committing suicide. Do you concur, Marshal?"

The Marshal remained silent.

Maxmillian pressed. "Might I inquire, Marshal, as to your response should the Americans, the Federalists I mean, attack us? Would France back me as promised?"

Again, total silence.

"Well, regardless. The Mexicans would never share the field with slavers. Absorption of them into our ranks would be a move so heinously despised we might as well ask the Mexican loyalists to defect."

"You're correct about that, Your Excellency." Bazaine said. "The Confederates are certain to seek that one way or another. I can tell you from our experience in Saint Domingue, what the negroes call Haiti, that slaves, once freed, will die rather than accept the yoke of human bondage again. Not a French man was left alive after the negro rebellion and Napoléon I, who was busy conquering Europe, could do nothing to save them or reassert control. Slavery is dying in the Americas and we should not fight this."

"A very erudite answer, Marshal. So we'll deny these Americans' offer of military assistance and make them disband."

The Marshal shrugged noncommittally.

"But we must find productive channels for their industriousness." Maximillian said. "Men who sacrifice so much to uphold a principle are men of resolute character and deserve our respect and support. We shall invite these men to integrate themselves into the colony at Carlota, named after my wife. Look at the fine leaders we have incorporated into our society – like Commodore Matthew Fontaine Maury, the world's premier oceanographer who helped lay the transatlantic cable and whose navigation charts are models of excellence.

"Now he serves as imperial commissioner of immigration, responsible for recruiting dissatisfied Americans to come settle in the Carlota colony. And General John Blankhead Magruder, the Confederate fighting man who acts as imperial commissioner of the land office whose idea it was to found Carlota in the first place! Half a million acres of arable land midway between Puebla and Veracruz, fertile for cotton, sugar and coffee. Offered for a dollar twenty-five per acre with six hundred forty acres to men with families and three hundred twenty to bachelors to settle homesteads. These Confederates will be instrumental in the rebuilding of the country."

"Oui. You're right, Emperor. Now I have something to say. Soon we'll have to issue the edict we've talked about for the cancellation of the right to trial. Our gallows are overflowing and the time and men spent in transporting guerrillas back to cities and then the cost of processing them cannot be borne any longer. Summary field executions will start soon, whether we want this or not."

Maximilian looked aghast.

"We mustn't do that! They will loathe us! To revoke any semblance of legal rights of my subjects? Too severe. We must find alternatives."

"There are no alternatives and this is not open for debate. I'm just advising you so you are prepared to sign the documents when the time comes. We have dallied for far too long on this matter."

The Emperor was speechless. There was nothing he could do or say; the French always got their way. This had been discussed for some time but it appeared reality now. Soon it would be fait accompli – the questions was whether he endorsed it or not. If he didn't, the French would still enact it and then move to replace him. If he signed, he would be responsible for more blood. How would he explain himself before God on the Day of Judgment?

September 5, 1865

In the capital, word had spread quickly of the Emperor's reply to the newly arrived Americans and his command for them to disband immediately. When it was announced that they would perform one final mustering ceremony the streets were abuzz with the news.

Just before noon, General Shelby led the remnants of the Iron Brigade into the Alameda Central. Around the fringes and from the windows hundreds of spectators observed the event. It was a beautiful, clear day.

The men, in full dress regalia, entered in single file alongside their horses. At the sound of the bugle, they fell into ranks for final inspection. Shelby passed by every single soldier, shaking his hand and briefly recalling a mutually shared moment of peril. Soldiers may not always be needed but they will always be soldiers.

One of the men, when spoken to by Shelby, began to weep unabashedly. Shelby paused and the two placed their heads together and rested a hand on each other's neck. It is thus when a man prepared to die for a cause learns the cause itself has died. Bereft, only sorrow remains.

The Emperor had been magnanimous in declining their help. Those who wished to remain were encouraged to join the Confederate community at Carlota. Those who did not, were to be granted free passage out of the country, to the extent the imperial authorities could ensure this.

Marshal Bazaine had given each of the men fifty dollars. They had played a role, but as actors that had not been called back. Their time on stage was finished. Time to exit.

At an order the standard-bearer ignited their flag. Never more would the Fourth Missouri Cavalry ride as a fighting unit.

The brigade bugler sounded another note and General Shelby swung onto his horse. He issued the order to mount and the men climbed on their horses in unison. The cavalrymen passed before their fascinated audience, first at a walk, then a canter.

As they approached the far corner of the Alameda Shelby cried, "Give'em hell boys!" and took off at a full gallop, letting loose a rebel yell. His men galloped and yelled with him and with a last show of bravado the Iron Brigade exited the stage, defiant to the end.

THE STARS AND STRIPES

January 5, 1866

At Miravelle, Emperor Maximilian was describing to his secretary,
José Blasio, the extravagant ball they had thrown at the palace to
celebrate the New Year. He was seated in his office on a two-person
chair with the backs inverted in an S-shape so that the two occupants
would sit facing one another as they conversed. His feet were propped
on a cushioned stool, and he had a pan of hot coals resting on his
belly, warming his body through a blanket.

José was seated nearby and was taking down whatever the
Emperor dictated. The ceremony had been grand indeed: punch
served from massive receptacles that you could almost bathe
in, mariachi bands performing, and a sumptuous feast served.
Maximilian was dictating a letter to an acquaintance in Vienna when
there were footsteps outside the office and the door opened abruptly.
It was Marshal Bazaine, unannounced and uninvited.

"Your Excellency, I must speak with you at once." The Marshal
was speaking French.

"Oui. I am free." Maximilian replied, having to change gears linguistically on sudden notice.

"The matter is confidential." Marshal Bazaine motioned to Secretary Blasio with his head unabashedly, not deigning to look directly at him.

Maximilian lifted his hand and Blasio closed up the letter, lifted the wooden writing panel he had come in with, and excused himself.

Maximilian placed his coal pan on the floor, and the Marshal stepped into the center of the room, remaining standing while the Emperor reclined.

"Yesterday American soldiers attacked the garrison of the town of Bagdad, near Matamoros." Bazaine said. "Your soldiers were taken prisoner and are now in Texas. One of our ships tried to approach and was fired upon by their artillery. It withdrew undamaged."

Maximilian could feel his face flushing with rage.

He burst out, "I won't stand for this! An invasion? An attack on my sovereignty?"

Indignant, he leapt up from the couch and began to pace energetically.

"Well, we'll need more troops then, from France I mean. And we'll declare war unless they offer full compensation and a public apology."

"I don't believe that is a practical posture, Your Excellency."

"Not practical? Impractical?" Maximilian was beside himself with incredulity.

"The United States is not an enemy we can afford to have, my Emperor. And might I remind you of our troubles at home?" Bazaine's voice trailed and he seemed to incline his head slightly as he said this. "Lastly, they are merely trying to provoke us into declaring war."

"We haven't any choice. This was forced upon us. The world will sympathize. Emperor Napoléon will just have to send more troops, Marshal Bazaine."

Looking directly into Maximilian's eyes Bazaine said "I doubt that will be his decision."

"It must be his decision. He has committed to me to follow this through until the end. The situation has changed. We need additional men."

"Yes, well, Emperor, certainly. I shall include your request in my communiqué to His Highness, Napoléon III and will advise you of his position. However, my council is to begin to search for alternative solutions."

"It is not a request. It is –" Maximilian stopped as if he had been slapped. An expression of utter shock on the part of Bazaine had made him hesitate.

An awkward moment of silence occurred and then Marshal Bazaine said curtly "Good day, Your Excellency," and walked out the door briskly, leaving Maximilian in an opulent study in a beautiful castle on a hill in a country very far from his homeland – utterly alone.

August 1866

Juan Antonio peered over the loose stone wall surrounding the farm. There were eight foreign soldiers approaching: French, Belgian, Austrian, or Arab. It had become impossible to predict nowadays – anything went in the French foreign legion.

He signaled for his men to remove their brimmed sombreros and began to knead the upturned part of the brim of his own in his hands. This was a habit he had developed to release the nervous energy that he felt at times like this since assuming command of the ten men with him.

Garcia also had taken command of a small group and consequently they fought separately.

It was late in the day and the soldiers approaching them were returning to town.

Juan Antonio and his men had watched them leave on patrol around noon, and now they were going to spring their trap as they came back, tired and careless. It was foolish of them to venture out beyond the garrison, for the Mexicans controlled all of the surrounding area.

The summer heat was making his legs sweaty under the leather leggings most of the men wore. He looked over at his group: ten hardened men all confident and eager to fight. He even had an Irishman who had come down to join their cause after fighting for the army of the northern United States. The remainder were all Mexicans either from the region or who had been fighting for longer than one year.

How far they had come from those desperate days in Puebla over three years ago! His hero, General Jesús González Ortega, had fallen from grace with Juárez and had been declared in dereliction of his duties while in the United States garnering support for their cause. There had been rumors that he had sought foreign backing for his own presidency in México after the war, which was not far off. The fallen hero of Puebla.

This had made Juan Antonio very sad, but in the past four years Juan Antonio had grown to be his own man and he was proud of what he had grown into. Resignation to tragedy had merely been one more step in maturation.

Across the country the French forces were receding: Chihuahua, Guadalajara, Matamoros, Tampico, Acapulco, Monterrey, and Saltillo had all been recaptured or evacuated by the French. The tide was turning.

The enemy soldiers were drawing closer now.

Juan Antonio ducked down behind the wall and shifted one of the stones so he could peer out at them. Only half their number looked French; the rest appeared to be central European. When they were close enough the men would all rise up and fire a volley. Two of the men, because they did not have repeating rifles, only muzzle loaders, would hold their fire. If the enemy soldiers wished to surrender as they often did now, they would permit this. They had won over a certain number of recruits this way.

The brutality of the Black Laws, or the waiver of all rights of the Mexicans to a representative trial had generated such hatred that even some of the French forces found themselves sympathizing with the Republicans.

When they were close enough all of the men stood and eight of them fired at close range. They were so near their targets that the thuds of bullets in flesh were audible and they knew one volley would be sufficient. Within seconds, six of the enemy soldiers had fallen and one of the remaining men was clutching his upper arm, his rifle beside him on the earth.

"Laissez vos armes." Juan Antonio commanded.

The one unwounded soldier let his rifle fall to the ground and unfastened his belt, leaving the knife and ammunition hanging from it.

Juan Antonio's men started to approach the French while the two who had not fired stood and trained their rifles on the remaining enemies. Juan Antonio drew a double shot derringer from his pants and walked toward the wooden gate in the wall. The two soldiers were staring at Juan Antonio plaintively. Their lives were in his hands. What if he were to treat them as they had treated his own people for the last four years?

One was French, the other unknown.

Juan Antonio spoke to the foreign mercenary. "Sprichst du Deutsch?"

"Ja," came the reply "nicht schiessen."

Austrian, or from one of the Germanic states. Well, the man need not worry – he wouldn't shoot.

"Strip the soldiers of their weapons, and if the survivors want, they can come back with us to camp." Juan Antonio said to his men. "Otherwise release them so they can relate what happened here. With the dead - put a sombrero over the faces of the French soldiers."

Juan Antonio enjoyed doing this to remind the French of the terrible enemy they had awakened. México City grew closer day by day.

DROWNING MEN WILL GRAB SWORDS

October 1866

Maximilian crept down the hall toward the exit. He moved stealthily to evade detection and was not wearing his medals or boots. None of his servants must witness him entering the carriage house.

The autumn sun shone in the corridor from the glass-paned doors as he walked by the marble-topped wall table with the portrait of the Empress suspended above it.

He wondered how Charlotte was. Her letters from Europe were unintelligible at times and raving always. Austrian nobles gossiped she was losing her sanity. Her diplomatic mission to Europe to elicit support for his empire had so far been unfruitful, even at the tables of his own relatives! That his own mother and brother should abandon them here!

Poor Charlotte! She was young and their existence was crushing her. She even wrote that his mother had lambasted her for decisions she felt were mistaken. How could they know over there, surrounded by the frivolous comforts of a decadent monarchy?

Slipping out the door, he moved quietly to the carriage house. He stepped inside and had to wait while his eyes adjusted to the darkness. None of the servants were there but, as arranged, the hired carriage was present and the side door was open. Marshal Bazaine gestured from the interior for him to come inside.

They had requested this secret meeting, because they could not discuss in the audience chambers what they felt needed to be said and with the frankness the circumstances required. What etiquette and their servants' curiosity curtailed in the audience room, they would confront in the carriage house.

Inside were the Marshal, the French ambassador Danot and the personal aide-de-camp of Louis-Napoléon, General Francois de Castelnau, who had recently arrived. As Maximilian entered, they gruffly exchanged greetings then the Marshal launched the dialogue.

"Nobody saw you come here?"

"No, not that I saw." Maximilian responded.

"Good. Well, we'll start then."

General Castelnau spoke "Emperor, you know I came from France to convey the personal wishes of Emperor Louis-Napoléon to your ah… attention."

The carriage was quite cramped with the four men, and Maximilian felt the weight of their stares and knew they meant to pressure him once more. He shifted on the felt cushion. Castelnau continued. "We cannot express the extent to which the Emperor desires you to abdicate the throne. You cannot maintain the interest payments and it has been months since we paid the troops a regular salary. This farce cannot be kept up any longer and we can no longer petition you politely."

Maximilian fired back angrily.

"I cannot pay the troops because you demand half of my revenue."

"Correct, Your Excellency." Ambassador Danot interjected. "Yet even though you doubled taxes, then doubled them a second time, your intake diminishes as you lose ground to the rebels. As you cannot pay the taxes, you lose yet more land to them. It's a vicious spiral and is – I implore you to acknowledge – untenable."

"It is not untenable. I just need more time and soldiers. You should finish what you started here. Who will collect your precious interest if I abdicate? They'll close the London Mexico Bank the day I leave."

No one replied.

Marshal Bazaine broke the silence.

"Last week we had reported – and I stress reported, not actual – desertion totals of up to seventy soldiers a day from the Legion. Your Excellency, nobody believes this war can be won anymore. This is your last chance to work with us. After all, every Frenchman in your cabinet has resigned by now. We are your last hope."

"Well, we all know the Legion Etrangère is just a motley collection of rabble: criminals hunted in their own land without any other option." Maximiliian retorted. "Moreover, we should cut off the rebels' support from the United States. Everyone knows they harbored Juárez in San Antonio. We should have declared war on them after they attacked us."

The three Frenchmen looked at one another then Ambassador Danot spoke.

"Your Excellency, you comprehend as well as we do that declaration of war was not a plausible option. We're beseeching you to be reasonable."

Maximilian spoke very crisply, enunciating every word. "I am being perfectly reasonable. I am being perfectly reasonable because I know what you'll have without me." He pointed his finger at the men in turn. "Nothing."

"With all the military costs incurred to this point you won't even break even. And I know full well what I have without you. Nothing. I have no home to go back to, no future but the shame of my failures. No, your best option is to back me until I outlast these rebels, and then I'll pay you every centime you're owed from this country."

General Castelnau laughed lightly, not sincerely but in a manner that displayed contempt. "Your Excellency, even the most naïve optimist couldn't delude himself into believing that. Look," – the General leaned forward and held his hands out in front of him, palms toward Maximilian – "if you return to Austria-Hungary, you can live in peace. The Seven Weeks' War with Prussia is over. There's no future for you here. We're being blunt. Staying here will only deteriorate the situation and we cannot guarantee your safety."

The men fell silent.

Maximilian broke eye contact and looked out the carriage window at the dark interior of the carriage house. They didn't understand; he couldn't go back. His own family had nailed his coffin shut. His route of retreat was barricaded by the influence of the Hapsburgs in the European courts. And he certainly wouldn't be extorted like this, pressured in a carriage! He needed time to weigh his options.

Would they withdraw their troops entirely? Since the start of June they had begun to pull back, but would they pull out completely?

Maximilian finally spoke "Thank you gentlemen, for your visit. I will discuss this matter further with Marshal Bazaine at a later time. Now if you'll excuse me."

With that, he left the carriage. On his way out of the carriage house he spotted a coachman dressed in black hiding in the shadows. The coachman tipped his hat and said, "Bonjour." As the man raised his arm, Maximilian noticed the wooden butt of a pistol tucked into his belt.

Back in the carriage, General Castelnau said, "What do we do if he won't bend?"

"We expect him to." Ambassador Danot replied. "He's not bright but he must have the foresight to see what will happen if he doesn't. If he won't be amenable we must find someone who will be favorable to us and not seek to demolish entirely what we have established here. It will not be easy. The ultraconservatives who have united behind him know that if he abdicates they will be killed. As successors they would never be accepted; their image is stained with the blood of tens of thousands of executed Mexicans. But we may have a possible candidate, isn't that right, Marshal?"

"Yes. One of the Republican generals. His name is Porfirio Díaz, and I have opened lines of communication with him. If we can create a situation in which Presidente Juárez's legitimacy is questioned, we can install Díaz and he would continue to pay us to a limited extent. Again, it's just a possibility but we're pursuing it."

"Bon." General Castelnau said. "See what he amounts to. Let's go back to the embassy."

They opened the door and called the coachman to take them away from Miravelle.

February 13, 1867

Maximilian accepted the offer of a boost onto his horse. Even in the sun the temperature was chilly this morning.

On January 10th Marshal Bazaine had received unconditional orders for complete withdrawal from Mexico, leaving Maximilian alone with the Imperial Mexican Army. Eight days ago the citizens of the capital had watched the subdued departure of the French soldiers for Veracruz, from where they would embark in another month for home when every unit had assembled at the port.

The rebels occupied most of the north, moving into the towns after the French garrisons had left. There had even been talk of the French selling weapons and information to them!

Only Mexico City, Querétaro, Puebla, Orizaba and Veracruz remained under the Empire's control. Yet he did not believe all was entirely lost. There remained some hope as long as a core group of supporters held fast and he remained at the head of an army.

Besides, best to be rid of the French who had always dictated his actions. They who had now abandoned him and even attempted to negotiate with various rebels behind his back: Jesús González Ortega, Lerdo de Tejada, Porfirio Díaz, even Benito Juárez himself!

They thought that he did not know about their offer to General Díaz – to arm him and hand over French occupied territory to him in exchange for Maximilian and his most steadfast generals' heads?

Well, he Ferdinand Maximilian, would show them he was a Hapsburg to the last!

Maximilian realized he had been daydreaming too long; the troops would perceive his brooding as a sign of weakness. He turned his horse around to face the column of soldiers behind him – good men but too few. Eighteen hundred, with seventy-two hundred more awaiting them in Querétaro. They were in ranks of four with their officers accompanying them in the ranks. Those on horses would trot alongside. With their straight-brimmed sombreros or officers' hats and rifles resting on their left shoulders they looked very smart and determined. Their jackets were ornamented with a row of brass buttons on either side and their sombreros were threaded with multicolored patterns on the brim. They marched under the flag of Imperial Mexico – with the orange band replacing the green one of the former government.

Victory could still be within their grasp...

"Men, today we march to Querétaro. From there we will undertake the liberation of the sections of our country that have fallen to the rebels. We no longer have French support, but this has been what has clouded our cause from the very onset. Now, we fight as united Mexicans for the future of the Empire of Mexico. We who remain are the purists. Let us not falter in the face of our mission. We march north on my signal. Viva México!"

He spun his horse back to face away from the column of soldiers. With a last glance at the buildings around them the Emperor smoothed his beard and spurred his horse forward.

The army started its fateful march north to Querétaro.

AU REVOIR, MAXIMILIAN

March 12, 1867

Marshal Bazaine stared over the wooden railing of the flag ship at the port of Veracruz. The Tricolore fluttered loudly above him in the Gulf breeze.

This was it; the last of the troops and equipment were on board. Only the honorary rearguard remained, rowing toward one of the other ships with the flag they had unfurled on the docks to ceremoniously mark their departure. It would end as it had begun.

What a debacle! Three hundred sixty million francs wasted. That the Second Empire should have participated in this affair! The elite of the French armée slain fighting peasants with sombreros in nameless mountain passes. Not two months ago, Marshal Adolphe Niel had been appointed war minister and had embarked on an ambitious military reform program. First and foremost would be the defenses in the Rhine border states. The new long-range Chassepot rifle would serve as the base upon which to restructure their army to meet the rising threat from the east, the newly formed North German

Confederation. For the first time since 1815 the Germanic lands were ruled by Berlin, not Vienna, and they grew more aggressive every day; they spoke of a German empire led by Prussia, of domination of the Continent, of being the superior Europeans! And the army was strained by its commitments in Algérie also.

The Austrians had been soundly defeated by the Prussians last year at Königgrätz, inflicting forty-four thousand casualties in one battle! Now all of Europe feared them. A key opportunity to unite three to one against Prussia with Austria and Hanover had been missed and the Emperor was playing for time.

A renewed recruitment drive had been initiated and the colonial garrisons were being depleted for the defense of the homeland. Napoléon III had completed the withdrawal of troops from Rome, leaving in their place a legion dedicated to the defense of the Pope and Rome from Italian encroachment.

There remained only the Czar and Napoléon III who could check these Teutonic aggressors. Yet the Czar dithered and avoided confrontation – had his allegiance been bought by von Bismarck? Reports had reached him of Prussian promises to restore Russian access to the Mediterranean, denied by Britain and France after the Crimean War. Additionally, the Russians were on the verge of selling their holdings across the Bering Sea to the American secretary of state, William Seward.

More American expansion.

Would les Anglais entertain an alliance? The balance of power on the Continent was threatened.

One of the ship's officers broke his reverie. The rearguard had boarded.

"Nous sommes tous prets, Maréchal." They were ready for departure.

"Partons, alors." he replied.

The ship lifted anchor and began to sail away from the Mexican coast. What chaos they were leaving behind.

Au revoir, Maximilian. Bon courage!

What a pitiable fool Maximilian was. Just three days ago the Mexicans had closed the noose around him in Querétaro. The empire that had been born of a desperate siege would die with one. Now that the French withdrawal, in motion for many months, was complete there would be no escape. The Mexican Conservatives had beguiled him into remaining, a mistake that would certainly mean his life. It would be the guillotine for him!

Black storm clouds had gathered in the north. The guerrillas, equipped by the Americans and cognizant of the French evacuation, had grown bolder by the day. The entire north had fallen into their hands. There had been no stopping this wave. Deprived of the northern cities and the accompanying revenue, Maximilian's house of cards would soon collapse. When the gold stopped coming in his army would abandon him. It was simply a matter of counting the days.

France's own diplomatic subterfuges had not met with success either. Proposed at the last minute and conducted from a position of utter desperation they had been unable to sway any of the Republican generals over. Soon this country would belong to Benito Juárez once again.

Sighing, he looked out at the Gulf of Mexico. The white crests slapped against the wooden hull of their ship and sea gulls hovered overhead curiously. Well, at least they had left with dignity. He descended the short flight of steps from the deck to his cabin and entered the room, closing the door behind him – and on the Europeans' last chance to stop the United States' rise to power and on the last attempt to re-impose European colonialism in the Americas.

LIFE IS NEVER BLACK AND WHITE

June 1867

"You can come up now. The Presidente will see you." The valet turned and Juan Antonio followed him through the courtyard and up the stairs of the Palacio del Gobierno of San Luis Potosí. It felt great to be back.

México's war for independence from France was over. "Emperor" Maximilian was to be executed in a few days in accordance with the decree emitted during the negotiations at La Soledad – a traitor to the Mexican nation.

The man who had ordered thousands of his countrymen hung or shot would finally receive his due punishment. Cornered in Querétaro for over three months and betrayed in the end by one of his own colonels, Colonel Lopez, for the sum of thirty thousand dollars in gold, Maximilian had surrendered to General Mariano Escobedo. The despised traitors of the nation, Miramón and Márquez, awaited the same fate.

The valet stopped at the wooden door and knocked. Juan Antonio recognized the Presidente's voice grant them permission to enter and Juan Antonio turned the handle and stepped through.

Juárez was seated on a sofa on the right side of the room. It was a small antechamber, a receiving room for the Presidente's guests. He rose and smiled at Juan Antonio, extending his hand.

"Hola, Juan Antonio. Como estas?"

"Muy bien, Señor Presidente. Thank you for seeing me."

"Not at all. How is your father?"

"He's well, thank you. He and the old group have started to gather at the Hotel America again but it's not the same without Señor Santiago as the owner."

"Yes, a tragedy. His example of resistance shall be remembered by us all."

The two deliberately observed a moment of silence before continuing.

"Juan Antonio, come with me. I want to leave this room and clear my head. You would not believe the visitor I just received."

Juárez stood and they opened the door on the far side of the room. They stepped into a large wooden floored library with paintings and sketches hanging on the walls.

"Muy bonito." Juan Antonio said, admiring the beauty.

"Yes, the French did maintain this room in good order. You know, not ten minutes ago I had to sit through the plea of an American woman, a Mrs. Salm Salm, who is married to one of Maximilian's closest associates. Can you imagine? There are norteamericanos saying we are being too tough on him, that we should show clemency, the man who brought us hell for three years. I say we should execute Napoléon of France while we're at it! But as I'm sure you've learned in life by now my young friend, there is always someone waiting to criticize..." Juárez let his voice trail off.

"I can't believe that. A norteamericano pleading for Maximilian's life? After all their condemnations of his government and support of ours?"

"Yes, well apparently she was a "Princess" no less… Pues, the situation is that the French rule is over and the norteamericanos have been our allies, so we have to overlook trivialities such as these."

The two men walked over to a writing table in the corner near a window that looked out upon the Plaza de Armas.

"Sit down. Tell me what's on your mind."

Juan Antonio pulled out the chair from the table and seated himself before the Presidente.

"Señor Presidente. I want to know what happened with Jesús Ortega."

"Ahhh…" Presidente Juárez looked away from Juan Antonio and stared out at the plaza, evidently uncomfortable.

He took a deep breath.

"General Ortega, like me, is a man who deeply loves his country. He has made countless sacrifices for it, and for that we are grateful. But sometimes when an individual loves something, he can love excessively. That love can cloud his judgment, make him possessive."

He hesitated and fiddled with a paperweight holding down a small stack of letters on the desk.

"I'm sure you have heard rumors and those always get exaggerated. General Ortega was charged with dereliction of his duties as a general while he was in the United States. The Congresso and I felt that he stayed in the United States to negotiate with both the norteamericanos and the French for personal position, and in any case, he was greatly overdue back home to fight the French! There were even allegations that he considered denouncing my rule and allying himself with the French. But, at the very end, the French were desperately offering anything to anyone they felt could save them, including me. They tried to parley with me – unsuccessfully of course – so I'm not sure if these accusations have much basis for credibility. So, he was not the only one, but he was one of the most loved, and thus was one of the most painful."

Juan Antonio felt more emotional than he had expected. Childhood dreams die hard.

"So he is in prison now, in the Bishop's prison in Monterrey. But, Juan Antonio, when you are at my level, you see constantly the effect power can have on people. Good men can do bad things and this does not condemn a man's soul to evil. I, too, have been tempted at times. Somewhere in his heart, I'm sure he believed what he was doing was what was best for México. However, that was not his decision to make.

"There was much confusion in the final days, and legitimately under the Carta Fundamental he would have been presidente when my term expired, but he chose to overlook the decree of the eighth of November, 1865 that prolonged my powers as head of state on an emergency basis. This measure was meant only to carry us through the war. Soon there will be elections again."

Juan Antonio nodded, still somewhat choked up.

"I know what a mentor he was to you, and he always spoke to me of your intrepidness and patriotism. I think that the Mexican nation will forgive her errant son to whom she owes so much. But again, that is not up to me."

"Did he really talk to the French?"

Presidente Juárez nodded. "I'm sure as enemies. Yet when he declared himself a candidate for presidente, he did so with clandestine French backing. And he was not the only one."

Now it was Juan Antonio's turn to gaze out the window at the Plaza de Armas. In six years so much had changed. That simple plaza, his innocent life, the friends that were now gone. Juan Antonio felt as if this revelation had killed his last link to his boyhood innocence and the existence he had known before the invasion.

Abruptly he had a vision of himself six years prior, running to this same plaza, stopping to talk to Graciana and hearing the announcement of the assassination of Melchor Ocampo. What a young boy he had been! How filled with the passions of youth and aspiring deeply to arrive at his own self estimation of manhood! Now here he sat before the leader of his nation, a respected patriot for his country. It was a journey from which he could not turn back now matter how hard he tried. Suddenly he realized how much he resented the French for having taken his youth from him.

Looking out the window at the townspeople crossing the plaza, Juan Antonio wondered how long it would have lasted – he a young man growing up in San Luis Potosí without the war. Would he have been able to retain his childhood innocence longer?

Suddenly he realized he had been staring pensively out the window for some time and that Presidente Juárez had fallen silent. He looked back at the Presidente and Juárez leaned forward, folding his hands.

"This is a time for forgiveness now. The war is finished and we must rebuild. I know you long for what was lost but now we must heal México, one day at a time." He smiled warmly.

"Yes, Señor Presidente. Thank you. Thanks for telling me."

"You deserved the full story. I know he was like a father to you. Remember that even good men do bad things, Juan Antonio. Heal and forgive."

The two men shook hands and said good-bye and Presidente Juárez sat down to continue rebuilding México, one day at a time.

June 19, 1867

It was still dark when Maximilian heard the men coming for him in his cell. The priest, Father Sofia, was a kind man who had offered him solace in these final hours through his gentle words and prayer, stood up and moved to the door.

It was time; six thirty in the morning. Today would be the last day of his life.

The keys turning in the metal lock of the reinforced door were very noisy and something about that sound almost drove him to faint. These bars which had imprisoned him in the solitary cell between the hallway and the courtyard of the Convent of Santa Cruz in Querétaro had come to represent his protection from the forces driving his pending execution. His countless entreaties to Benito Juárez had fallen on deaf ears as had those of the international community. Pushed to the end, Maximilian preferred the dimness of the cell to the everlasting darkness.

The priest walked with him to the carriages that would transport him, as well as Miramón and Mejía, to the Hill of the Bells, west of town. The sun had risen and every church bell in the town tolled the tidings of the approaching execution.

Leading before the cortege of three carriages were perhaps eighty men, most on foot but someone horseback. These men wore all black uniforms with matching black hats secured by straps. Only their sword belts were white. Behind the carriages approximately three hundred soldiers marched to guard and flank the procession.

The cortege made its way through the streets before the eyes of the multitude.

Maximilian straightened his beard and made sure his jacket fit snugly. The only thing he had left was his dignity. He could at least carry that to the grave. And, the officer had promised to let him speak his final words.

They arrived at the hill and stepped out of the carriages.

The hill was surrounded on all sides by thousands of soldiers. At the top of the hill was a wall with three crosses embedded in the earth in front of it. As he drew closer, Maximilian saw that each cross bore one of their names.

His old allies, Generals Miguel Miramón and Tomas Mejía, were being marched up the Hill of Bells now from the carriages. They who had fulfilled their vow to follow him to the death would justly join him in his fate.

A tremendous sense of betrayal lay over him. All this time, he had merely been a pawn for the French emperor who had abandoned him when conflict loomed with the North German Confederation over the succession to the Spanish throne. Abandoned by the French military which had profiteered from selling their weapons to his enemies as they left the country; abandoned by the Pope, who had been the first to wish him success; abandoned by his own family, the Hapsburgs of Austria-Hungary, who had denied him permission to return to the fold and who had disowned him entirely. His own mother and brother preferred that he die in this country rather than taint the honor of the Hapsburg line.

Even Charlotte had abandoned him, albeit unintentionally, by suffering a mental collapse. Did she understand, lost in her broken, paranoid state, back in her brother's castle that her husband would die? *Alas, poor Charlotte!* She would be the only one hurt by his departure. He was sad to leave her.

How could he have been so blind? All his efforts to bring enlightened monarchy to these people had been for nothing and he had been nothing more than a puppet for Louis-Napoléon of France. He could not meet the eyes of his allies. All of their support had been for personal gain. The Mexicans were right – they were butchers.

The guard escort formed a line in front of them and the priest distanced himself. Maximilian's breath grew short and the finality of the moment struck him dumb. Would the officer ask? A cloud passed overhead, and then the full light of the sun struck the three condemned men. This would be his last time to feel the sun's rays on his face.

The men came to attention and the officer walked along their ranks once to inspect them.

Maximillian's throat grew tight. His words would be the last essence of his life, his legacy in this world. Would the officer ask?

"You may say your final words." the officer said.

Relief swept over Maximilian. They were going to allow him a final expression of his being, something to be remembered by! Whatever his mistakes, he could leave some meaning to be remembered by.

"I give my life for a just cause, that of Mexican independence and liberty. May my blood which is about to be shed be for the good of my new country. Viva México!"

The words didn't seem to have much impact on his observers yet in his heart he was free.

"Preparan." the officer commanded.

The soldiers shouldered their rifles.

"Apuntan."

"Fuego!"

THE SAN PÉDRO HILLS

July 25, 1867

Juan Antonio and Garcia looked out over San Luis Potosí. They had climbed the San Pédro hills like they used to, as boys, ages ago. Now they had both scheduled to take a day of rest together to reminisce. The sun beat down on them and even the breeze and the elevation could not offset its effects.

"That's nice." Garcia said.

"Perfect." Juan Antonio was still a trifle winded.

Garcia removed his sombrero and wiped his brow. "I never really appreciated how serene it is up here. It's a gift."

"Yes." Juan Antonio said. "The French burned a lot of the houses but they didn't burn them all. The old center is still intact. You can really see what survived and what didn't from this height." He looked around at the rocky, scrub-brush hills. "It's not the same though. This, I mean. We're not kids anymore."

Garcia stared directly at Juan Antonio. "No it's better. And we never broke our vow."

"We did have to separate," Juan Antonio replied "but that doesn't matter. It just seems distant now, like something from a dream – yet a dream that we woke up from forever changed. Sometimes I want to go back to the life I had before the dream."

"They say you can never cross the same river twice." Garcia said. "The war changed us – it changed everything. Many of our friends are gone, but for the first time in history México stood up. This was our land and they tried to take it. But we saved it for ourselves and for our children. This is our legacy."

Below them they could discern a man repairing a corral fence. Life had returned back to normal fairly quickly.

"What a situation now between Juárez and Díaz!" Juan Antonio said. "I mean, after Juárez's triumphal entry into México City ten days ago, when he snubbed Díaz, who had come out to greet him as if he were handing the city to Juárez. What a popularity act!"

"Yes. Everyone sees it for what it was though. Díaz just thirsts for the top seat. Juárez can suppress him though." Garcia said. "By the way, you've been talking with Graciana all the time."

"Oh yes, just in passing."

"Well you pass her pretty often. You two should get married you know."

Juan Antonio smirked self-consciously. "Me? Us?" he asked. "You're the handsome one."

The men laughed together and looked out over San Luis Potosí.

"It's better without the war." Juan Antonio said. "México is free to build her future."

And the mountain breeze blew through the San Pédro hills down over the town of San Luis Potosí.

Postscript

Charles-Louis-Napoléon Bonaparte III was humiliatingly defeated with his generals by the Prussians on September 1st, 1870 in Sedan, France. He was captured and the Second Empire died. It was replaced by the Third Republic, which deposed Napoléon III, and still lost the Franco-Prussian War, consequently ceding Alsace and Lorraine. The North German Confederation became the German Empire. Historians say the depletion of the French army in Mexico greatly contributed to this defeat. Napoléon III died in exile in Chiselhurst, England January 9th, 1873.

The French supreme military commander who was blamed in allowing his troops to be surrounded and isolated at Metz, requiring rescue, which subsequently led to the disastrous battle of Sedan, was Achille Francois Bazaine. After the war – based on accusations he had conspired with the Prussians to be a puppet emperor who would cede Alsace and Lorraine – he was convicted of treason but escaped and spent the rest of his life in Spain and Italy. Enmity between Bazaine and Napoléon III factored heavily into Bazaine's inaction in that war, as the Emperor had laid the blame for the Mexican fiasco on Bazaine's shoulders after the withdrawal, a move than Bazaine never forgave him for.

To this day the flags of the French foreign legion have "CAMERONE 1863" sewn on them and April 30th, Camerone Day, is observed in honor of the legionnaires who died there. That event is viewed as the catalyst that changed the French foreign legion from a random collection of foreign mercenaries into a serious, determined fighting force.

Jesús González Ortega was released from prison on August 1st, 1868, and reentered public service on July 11th, 1869. He was named special envoy and minister to Spain on March 11th, 1874, and on January 6th, 1881, he was reinstated to the rank of general. He died on February 28th, 1881.

Benito Pablo Juárez Garcia continued to hold the presidency until his death, July 18th, 1872. It was a time of continued turmoil and poverty in Mexico because foreign investment credit was suspended, as were diplomatic relations with most of Europe. There were various challenges to his authority, the most serious posed by General Porfirio Díaz. Upon his death Benito Juárez left a sum equivalent to multiple millions in today's money to his wife – a fact that was very poorly viewed, because at the time of the end of French rule in 1867 he had been penniless. Regardless of the controversy, he was president of Mexico for fourteen and a half years and will always be loved and admired as the man who struggled ceaselessly to build a better Mexico.

Maximilian's body was returned to Trieste January 16th, 1868, on the same ship that he had traveled to Mexico in, and then forwarded to its final resting place in the imperial crypt in Vienna. He is viewed as a tragic figure in history.

Marie-Charlotte-Amélie lived a nondescript life in Europe until her death on January 16th, 1927.

The United States, true to Europe's worst fears, eclipsed European hegemony within fifty years after the end of the French intervention in Mexico – a fact measured among other factors, by its surpassing England in maritime power and economic clout, as well as being able to help bring the Allies to victory over the Central Powers in the First World War.

James Dunwoody Bulloch, after a largely successful career buying ships for the Confederacy, was denied amnesty by the United States, and lived out the remainder of his life in Liverpool, England. He died on January 7th, 1901.

Thomas Jefferson Page was able to cross the Atlantic, despite being hounded by Union ships and turned the *Stonewall* over to Spanish authorities in Cuba on May 19th, 1865, for sixteen thousand dollars in cash to pay his crew's salary. The Spanish subsequently turned it over to the United States government, which in turn sold it to the Japanese for their fledgling navy.

Joseph Orville Shelby remained with the Confederates in Mexico to work as a wagon-freight hauler and to farm the extensive Hacienda Santa Anna that he was granted, two miles outside of Cordoba. The hacienda was named for the previous owner, General Santa Anna de Lopez. After Maximilian's execution, Shelby was *persona non grata* with the Juárez government and he returned to the United States. There, he worked as a wheat farmer and in other pursuits, including holding the position of U.S. Marshal. He died on February 13th, 1897.

As for the rest of the men of the Iron Brigade, some dispersed to other parts of Latin America and Asia to serve as soldiers of fortune, some chose a side in the conflict and fought with either the French foreign legion or the Juaristas, and some settled in the Carlota colony. After the collapse of Maximilian's regime, those that had stayed were obliged to return to the United States.

José de la Cruz Porfirio Díaz first contested the legitimacy of Juárez's rule, then rebelled against it. Denied power twice democratically, first by Juárez then by his successor, Lerdo de Tejada, he deposed him and installed himself as an unbridled dictator, ruling despotically until 1911, when he was forced into exile.

And as for Juan Antonio Ayala, I couldn't find any more records on him. But I'd bet like most people who rise to circumstances beyond their control, he went on to live a happy, comfortable life in the country he had defended with his blood and sweat.

After all, isn't that what you'd do?

What If?

What if Mexico had not defended herself so tenaciously? What if her people had not stood their ground at Puebla both times? Would a French puppet regime in Mexico have been able to turn the tide of the American Civil War? Divided, would the United States have risen to the prominence it enjoys today? Would it be two separate countries? How would this have influenced events of the twentieth century? Would the rest of the Americas speak French?

What if Napoléon III had not reneged on his deal to sell the ironclads to the Confederacy? Would the Union blockade that strangled the Confederacy have been broken?

What if Maximilian had accepted the Confederates' offer to serve as his soldiers? Would the United States have invaded Mexico to uproot the ex–Confederates?

What if France had not lost their best troops in Mexico and had benefited from them in the fight against the North German Confederation? Would the German Empire have been created? Would there have been a First World War? Would there have been a Second World War? Would there have been a Cold War as the USSR was able to move into the vacuum left in Eastern Europe by Nazi Germany's collapse?

What if France had never invaded Mexico? Would Mexico have been able to get on its feet economically and not succumb to the thirty-five year dictatorship of Porfirio Díaz?

What if England had decided to move ahead with plans to attack the United States from Canada in the midst of the Civil War? Would the North have lost?

Bibliography

Rangel, Juan Jose Flores. *Historia de México*. Mexico City: International Thomson Editores, 2002.

Sánchez, Faustino Aquino & Murillo, Alfredo Hernández. *Las intervenciones extranjeras en México*. Instituto Nacional De Antropología Y Historia/Asociación De Amigos Del Museo Nacional De Las Intervenciones.

Belenki, A. *La intervencion francesa en México 1861-1867*. Mexico City: Edciones Quinta Sol, 1996.

Altamirano, Ignacio Manuel. *El Zarco*. Mexico City: Editores Mexicanos Unidos, 2002.

Black, Jeremy. *Atlas of World History*. London: Dorling Kindersley Limited, 1999.

Du Vignaud, Bertrand. *Monuments de France*. Bilbao, Spain: Chene, 1991.

Ledru, Eric. *Napoléon – Le Conquérant Prophétique*. Paris: Molière, 1995.

Boucicaut, Aristide. *Souvenir of a Visit to the Bon Marché*. Paris: Lahure, 1905.

Van Doren Stern, Philip. *The Confederate Navy A Pictorial History.* New York: Da Capo Press, 1992.

Edwards, John N. *Shelby's Expedition to Mexico.* Fayetteville: The University of Arkansas Press, 2002.

Rasgos del Golpe de Estado. Historical Archives of Mexico City, Mexico.

El Sitio de Pubela. Historical Archives of San Luis Potosí, Mexico.

Museum of the Mexican Army and Air Force, Mexico City, Mexico.

Museum of Foreign Interventions, Mexico City, Mexico.

Museums and Forts of Puebla, Mexico.

Museum of History, Monterrey, Mexico.

Museum del Palacio del Gobierno, San Luis Potosí, Mexico.

24477502R00147

Made in the USA
Lexington, KY
21 July 2013